CREATIVITY UNBOUND
An Introduction to Creative Process

Blair Miller
Jonathan Vehar
Roger Firestien
Sarah Thurber
Dorte Nielsen

5th edition, © 2011

For more information about training materials in creativity, innovation and problem solving, contact: info@foursightonline.com.

PUBLISHED BY FOURSIGHT, LLC, 1809 CENTRAL STREET, EVANSTON, IL 60201 USA

Table of Contents

Acknowledgments

The authors want to acknowledge the people and organizations who were indispensable in creating this manual:

Russ Schoen, Bill Shephard, Gerard Puccio and the International Center for Studies in Creativity at Buffalo State College.

5th Edition, Copyright © 2011 All Rights Reserved.
Miller, Vehar, Firestien, Thurber, Nielsen

Foreword (march!)

Ask someone—anyone—what they're mulling over. What has them stuck or frustrated or stressed? At any given moment in the life of a person, partnership or organization, there's always something: a problem, a challenge, a quandary. Something that's got us stumped. Something that's making us unproductive.

With all our collective years of education and experience, life still manages to pitch us curve balls that require new thinking and novel approaches. How do I shorten my two-hour commute? How do I spend more time with my kids? How can I lose 15 pounds? How can I get rid of these migraines? How can I take my husband on a surprise vacation? How can I finance my son's college education?

It's the same for organizations. Even the most profitable keep asking: How can we shorten the time to market? How can we boost profit margins? How can we organize ourselves for competitive advantage? How can we lead the market? But organizations often require groups of people to solve problems. Enter committees, teams, work groups, departments... And groups can be notoriously slow at getting to action.

That's where Creative Problem Solving (CPS) comes in. It provides a simple, repeatable way for groups—and individuals—to take on new challenges and come up with effective, even breakthrough solutions that have the benefit of everyone's input. The "magic" ingredient is creativity, people's innate ability to innovate, the natural instinct to come up with something new, to hit on something original that works. The rest is simply architecture—ground rules, techniques and road maps—that clear the way for creative solutions to surface.

There are two levels of Creative Problem Solving to master. The first is *Creativity Unbound: An Introduction to Creative Process.* That's all you need to participate in a CPS session or improve your own problem-solving ability. The second level is *Facilitation: A Door to Creative Leadership.* Here you learn to lead a group through a CPS session and help others improve their problem-solving abilities.

Our goal is to make you more effective at whatever aspect of creativity and problem solving excites you most and serves you best. Meanwhile, we've tried to keep it fun, simple and useful.

As you'll see, group feedback is essential to the process of coming up with creative breakthroughs, so if you have feedback for us, don't hesitate to share. It's all part of the process.

Welcome to the magic!

Blair Miller
Jonathan Vehar
Roger Firestien
Sarah Thurber
Dorte Nielsen

Please don't try this at home.

About the Authors

Blair Miller

Blair is founder and president of Blair Miller & Associates, a Chicago-based consulting and training firm that helps organizations deliver on their goals of creative leadership, team building and innovation. Blair is an Adjunct Professor of Creativity, Innovation and Change Leadership at SUNY's International Center for Studies in Creativity, and he serves as a guest instructor, teaching about innovation at MBA programs, including the Kellogg School of Management, University of Chicago, and Emory University. Blair has co-authored numerous articles and books on creativity and innovation. He is publisher of *FourSight: The Breakthrough Thinking Profile*, which offers individuals and teams the ability to see how their personal problem solving style affects their creative output.

Jonathan Vehar

Jonathan Vehar is a Senior Partner at New & Improved where he works with organizations to develop personal creativity and innovation for teams. *Investor's Business Daily* calls him "an Innovation Guru," and his quick wit, piercing insights and commitment to excellence create powerful programs in the areas of creative thinking, new product ideation, strategic planning, creative problem solving, and group meeting facilitation. He is a co-developer of the "Plain Language Creative Problem Solving" model and the author of many articles, video-tapes and training manuals about creative problem solving. His latest co-authored book is entitled, *"More Lightning, Less Thunder: How to Energize Innovation Teams."*

Roger Firestien, Ph.D.

Dr. Roger Firestien is President of Innovation Resources, Inc. and Associate Professor at the International Center for Studies in Creativity at the State University of New York College at Buffalo. He is the author of over 70 articles, books, audio and video programs published in both the popular and professional press. Some of his publications include: *From Basics to Breakthroughs, Power Think*, and the creativity fable, *Why Didn't I Think of That?* He is the host of the video programs, *Unleashing the Power of Creativity* and *Brilliant, Simply Brilliant!* He is publisher of the internationally recognized creativity newsletter, *Creativity That Gets Results*. His latest book, *Leading on the Creative Edge*, is in bookstores nationwide.

Sarah Thurber

Sarah is managing partner of FourSight LLC, a Chicago publishing company that develops research-based thinking tools that help teams and organizations innovate. For the past ten years, she has collaborated with top trainers and academics to help develop and market the company's flagship product, "FourSight the Breakthrough Thinking Profile." FourSight now sells a complete suite of innovation training tools in six continents and five languages. Sarah brings to FourSight a rich background in freelance writing, editing and graphic design. Her work has taken her on assignment to China, New Zealand and Italy. Sarah holds a Graduate Certificate in Creativity and Change Leadership from the International Center for Studies in Creativity, Buffalo, New York.

"So, how many post-it pads did you folks actually burn through to collaborate on this little book?"

Dorte Nielsen

Dorte is a head of department and a course leader of "Creative Communication" a BA education for Art Directors and conceptual thinkers at the Danish School of Media and Journalism, were she teaches creativity and creative thinking. Dorte is the author of numerous books and articles on creative thinking and in recent years held the position of Chairman of Creative Circle, the Danish society for the creative industries. For most of the 90's she worked as an Art Director in London. Her advertising work there won her recognition at the Cannes International Advertising Festival, D&AD, the British Television Awards, Epica, London International Advetising Awards, Campaign Poster Awards among others. Born in Denmark, Dorte Nielsen studied at The Graphic Arts Institute of Denmark and later at The School of Communication Arts in London. Dorte also holds a Graduate Certificate in Creativity and Change Leadership from the International Center for Studies in Creativity, Buffalo, New York.

Long, long ago, back in 1953...

A Little CPS History

Creativity kingpins

Creative Problem Solving (CPS) was invented—or perhaps it's more accurate to say, it was *discovered*—in the mid 1950's by a whole community of academics, thinkers, artists, inventors and business people. The truth is, everybody solves problems. Creative Problem Solving is simply a description of the stages people go through when they take on a problem for which they don't know the solution.

It took the genius of thinkers like Alex Osborn, an advertising executive, and Sidney Parnes, an academic researcher, to realize that making the problem-solving process explicit—rather than strictly intuitive—could help people improve their problem-solving abilities. It could help people come up with more creative solutions to problems. It could literally change the way people think.

The point is, Creative Problem Solving is powerful stuff. And it comes to you via years of dedicated study and research. We owe thanks, not only to Osborn and Parnes, but also to creativity kingpins like Ruth Noller, Morris Stein and E. Paul Torrance. (For a complete CPS timeline, see page 106.)

In addition to the ground-breaking work of those above, the authors would like to honor the institutions that have been steadfast in keeping the CPS flame burning, most notably the International Center for Studies in Creativity, in Buffalo, New York and the Creative Education Foundation (CEF), in Amherst, Massachusetts.

This book will introduce you to the tip of the creativity iceberg. To pursue the field of creativity further, flip through the appendix for more references, sources and growth opportunities.

Learning Objectives
The skills you'll acquire

Things you'll be able to do (better) after reading this book:

- Defer judgment when listening to a new idea

- Recognize when your creativity is being limited

- Overcome creative blocks

- Wield new tools that help you create options in the face of problems and challenges

- Master tools for judging options and making effective decisions

- Make detailed action plans for implementing strategies

- Get better at identifying potential resources that could help you sell your new ideas or solutions

- Use proper etiquette while diverging and converging

- Know where to put the red dot that indicates "You are Here" on the road map of any problem you're trying to solve

- Identify the characters on this page

- Find possibility in the face of challenge

Notes:

A Look at Creativity

"I do believe it is possible to create, even without ever writing a word or painting a picture, by simply molding one's inner life. That too is a deed."

ETTY HILLESUM

Bedrock Beliefs

Faith + Skills = More Creativity

The goal of this book is to help you be more creative. Part of that will involve mastering a few concepts, skills and techniques. But there's another equally important part to becoming more creative: You have to believe it's possible.

The Faith

That's why the first item on our agenda is to share our "Bedrock Beliefs" about creativity, listed below. We have a fundamental faith (based on thorough academic research) that everyone can be more creative, which is why we bother teaching these tools and techniques at all.

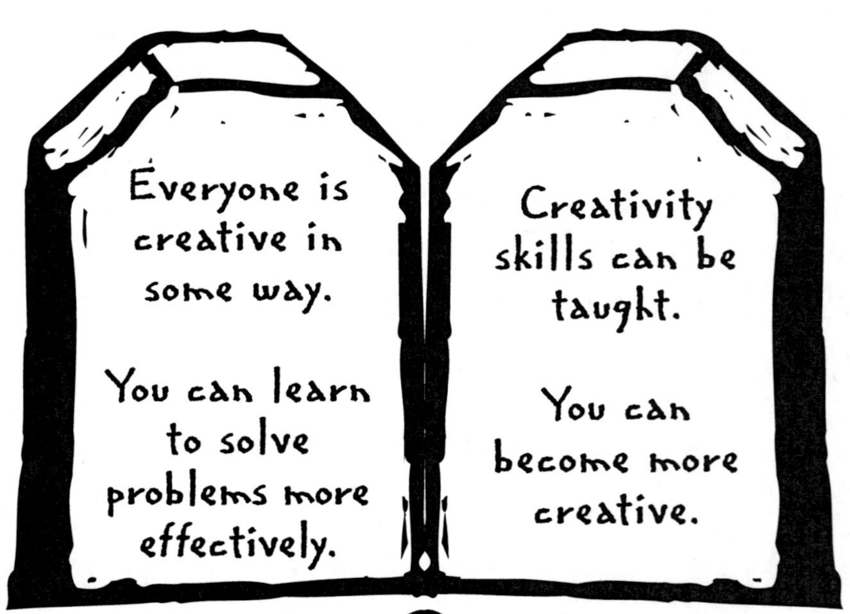

Bedrock Beliefs

In and Out Thinking

Around the world in 80 seconds

To help you get the most out of this book, we thought we'd share some research findings from the American Psychological Association. They studied what people do during a seminar, speech or workshop and found that at any given time:

18% are really listening to the presenter
25% are having erotic thoughts
57% are thinking about something else

This phenomenon is called "in and out thinking." Most people can speak about 150 words per minute, but they can hear and comprehend 900-950 words per minute. Because your mind thinks faster than people speak, you're only fully attentive during the first 13 to 18 seconds of any presentation, discussion or conversation. Then you fade out and think about other things.

Take "in" and "out" notes

Get this natural tendency to work in your favor. Draw a line down the center of your note paper. On the left side, record "in" thoughts: anything you want to remember from the presentation. On the right side, record "out" thoughts: any related ideas, new ideas or connections; the phone number of someone you need to call; something you have to remember to do; anything unrelated so you can free your mind to listen to the presentation.

This "in and out thinking" note-taking technique is designed to free you from trying to remember "out" thoughts and encourage you to generate new ideas without losing track of the presentation.

In and out thinking is nothing to be embarrassed about.

A Working Definition

You could spend a lifetime trying to define creativity, but in the interest of expedience, we'll start off with the definition set down by Stan Gryskiewicz of the Center for Creative Leadership in Greensboro, North Carolina. He defined creativity as follows:

Creativity = Novelty that's useful

Novelty: newness, originality, a fresh approach
Useful: serves a purpose, has value

More definitions of creativity...

"Ability to overcome self-imposed constraints."
AZKOFF & VERGARA (1988)

"The ability to see what isn't there, to recognize its power, and to make that power manifest."
THURBER & MILLER (2001)

"...becoming sensitive to or aware of problems, deficiencies, gaps in knowledge, missing elements, disharmonies and so on; bringing together available information; defining the difficulty or identifying the missing element; searching for solutions, making hypotheses and modifying and retesting them; perfecting them; and finally communicating the results."
E. PAUL TORRANCE & R.E. MYERS (1970)

"Creativity is the process of generating unique products by transformation of existing products. These products, tangible and intangible, must be unique only to the creator, and must meet the criteria of purpose and value established by the creator."
WELSCH (1980)

The Four P's

A model of creativity

Admittedly, some people chafe under a single, restrictive definition of creativity. After all, what about creative people? Creative products? Creative environments? Creative approaches? Creativity manifests itself in all kinds of ways, making it hard to settle on a universal definition or explanation.

Those looking for a more holistic approach will appreciate the work of Mel Rhodes, considered by some to be the Don Quixote of creativity. Mel set off on a personal quest to find an all-encompassing definition of creativity. He researched all the literature and collected definitions from myriad sources. Still, one single definition eluded him. Finally, he settled for describing creativity with the "Four P's."

Person = how people are creative; how creative someone is; the characteristics associated with creative people

Product = the artifacts of creativity; what is a creative product; what makes something creative; how can you tell if something is creative

Process = how people create or can use and apply their creativity (the primary focus of this book)

Press = the climate surrounding person, process and product, in which creativity flourishes or is squelched

> "... the definitions form four strands. Each strand has a unique identity academically, but only in unity do the four strands operate functionally."
>
> MEL RHODES (1961)

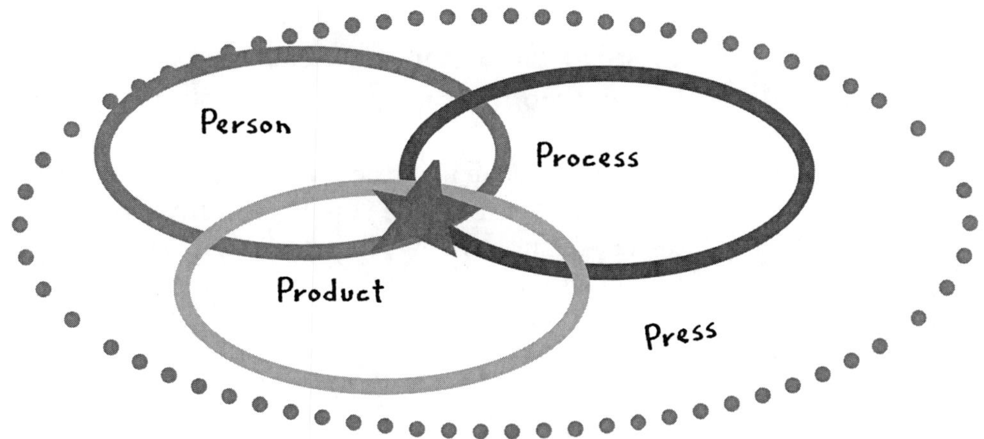

Creative Climate

The importance of "Press"

Remember that forth "P"—press? That's creative climate. Encourage a creative climate and watch the creative output of an individual, group, team or organization soar. Why? Organizational climate directly influences what people will do and how well they will do it. Theresa Amabile's research revealed that climate affects a person's *motivation* for a given task. And motivation is the key to creative performance. Look at it this way:

What you can do: *Determined by your content expertise and creativity skills* **What you will do:** *Determined by your motivation*
How well you will do it: *Depends on the type of motivation*

Two types of motivation:

Intrinsic: *Motivation to do something for its own sake (it gives you joy)*
Extrinsic: *Motivation to do something for an external goal (i.e. money, obedience, recognition, etc.)*

Creative climate promotes intrinsic motivation.
Intrinsic motivation promotes creative behavior.

When people are intrinsically motivated they pursue work with vigor and passion. Where are you intrinsically motivated? Think back over the last 12 months. Which projects did you perform your best on? What factors contributed to your success?

Stimulants and Obstacles to Creativity

What makes for a creative climate? Good lighting? Ergonomic furniture? In fact, research by Goran Ekvall reveals 10 dimensions (nine positive and one negative) that seem to have the greatest impact on a creative environment. With this awareness, we can take direct action to improve the climate for creativity.

9 Stimulants

What are you doing to deliberately make this dimension as good as it can be in your group, team, organization?

Challenge
The emotional involvement of the members of the organization in its operations and goals

Freedom
The independence in behavior exerted by the people in the organization

Idea Support
Ways new ideas are treated

Trust and Openness
The emotional safety in relationships

Dynamism and Liveliness
The eventfulness in the life of the organization

Playfulness and Humor
The spontaneity and ease that is displayed

Debate
Encounters and clashes between viewpoints, ideas, and differing experiences and knowledge

Risk Taking
The tolerance of uncertainty in the organization

Idea Time
The amount of time people can and do use for elaborating new ideas

1 obstacle

What are you doing to deliberately minimize the impact of these obstacles on your team, group, organization?

Conflict
The presence of personal and emotional tensions (in contrast to the idea tensions in the debate dimension) in the organization

Creativity Crushers

How do you treat new ideas? How are your ideas treated? Do you resist new ideas? How might you change this behavior?

Idea makers and breakers

What are the primary culprits when it comes to crushing creative thinking: habits, rules and traditions, perceptual blocks (comfort with the status quo), cultural blocks and conformity pressures, and emotional blocks such as fear of failure or being different. The next time you get "stuck"and need a creative breakthrough, ask yourself the following questions, designed to flex creative thinking:

How else can I do that?
What if..?
How can I use something that doesn't fit with this at all?

Monitor non-verbal messages

Start to monitor your non-verbal messages in day-to-day speaking and listening, when you work in groups and teams, when people are creating new options, when you're evaluating new concepts and when you're moving toward a new vision. Communication researcher, Dr. Albert Mehrabian, has researched the power of verbal and non-verbal communication. By his estimation:

Over 90% of both positive and negative meaning is conveyed by tone of voice and body language.

Praise to criticism ratio

Use praise to support people and ideas, rather than criticism to "correct" them. Studies in education show that it takes nearly a 4:1 praise-to-criticism ratio just to keep students on track.* Changing behavior requires an even higher praise-to-criticism ratio, about 8:1. When researchers analyzed how teachers actually tried to change student behaviors, they found the praise-to-criticism ratio was exactly the opposite, about one praise to four criticisms. Remember, praise can be a tool for positive change.

*Research on blocks to creativity adapted from Les Jones (1987) who developed and tested a psychological instrument to measure barriers to effective problem solving in his unpublished Masters thesis at the University of Manchester, UK. *Brown, W.E. (1972, May). Praise-Criticism Ratio: Do teachers take advantage of it? Behaviorally Speaking.*

The Triune Brain

...the lizard in you

Understanding the brain can bolster creativity. Here is a simplified (a very simplified) model of the brain. A more detailed description appears in Dr. Paul McLean's book The Triune Brain. *But in essence, the brain has three basic parts ...*

...the Brain Stem

At the core of our brains is the brain stem. McLean calls it the "reptilian brain" because it's essentially the same brain reptiles have. The reptilian brain figures out how to get food and not be food. It's about survival — both physical and psychological. It's about territory, protection, instinct and automatic action. The reptile's response to anything new is likely to be "attack it, run from it, eat it...or not even notice it."

...the Limbic System

Surrounding the brain stem is the limbic system which moderates hormones and other chemicals that affect our moods. It's the governing body for emotions. Chemicals here can make us sick or well, happy or frightened. The limbic system's motto: "feel, feel, feel."

...the Neo-cortex

Sitting atop the limbic system is the neo-cortex or "new brain." This is headquarters for speaking, thinking and problem solving. The neo-cortex is the learning brain — the source of creative thinking. It's motto is "learn, learn, learn and create, create, create."

Upshifting and Downshifting

According to Dave Meier, director of the Center for Accelerated Learning, you can shift into a creative mode by being conscious of "where" your thinking comes from. Threatening situations produce negative feelings. The limbic system actually releases chemicals that depress the thinking part of the brain. People automatically "downshift" into the reptilian brain. They react. A boss might tell employees, "Screw up, and you're outta here!" Imagine what kind of work environment this creates. Up shifting is thinking from the neo-cortex. When in need of new ideas, make a conscious "up shift" from the reptilian brain to the neo-cortex. Up shifting lets us learn, create and succeed.

> "A first-rate soup is more creative than a second-rate symphony!"
>
> MASLOW

Creative Product

What makes a creative product? Cool packaging? Hip name? Usefulness? While most people say they know a creative product when they see it, research by Susan Besemer, Donal Treffinger and Karen O'Quinn revealed that there are three explicit dimensions to a creative product.

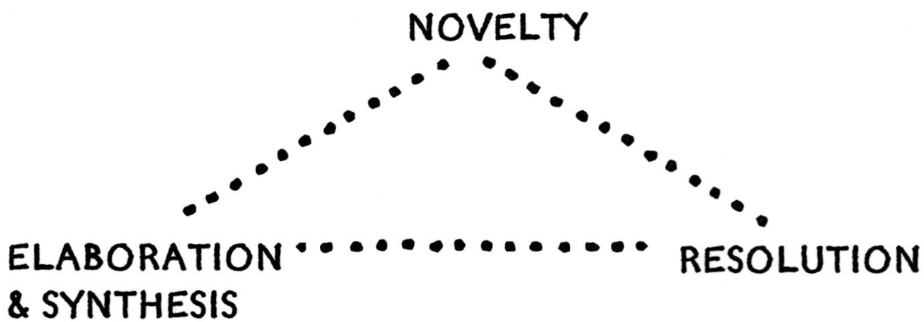

The Three Dimensions

A creative product is the outcome or artifact of a creative endeavor. It can be tangible or intangible — a new car or a new concept — but it's bound to display novelty, resolution and elaboration & synthesis.

Novelty: Is this product original in some way? Novelty is the degree of originality of the product in terms of new concepts, processes or new materials used. But beware, novelty alone does not guarantee a creative product. The madman who thinks himself a toaster may well utter a novel thought, but few would call it useful. So if novelty is not enough, what else does a creative product require?

Resolution: Does the product work? That is, how well does the product solve the challenge for which it was created. Is it useful? Does it provide value?

Elaboration & Synthesis: Is this product coherent? Elaboration & synthesis is the degree to which a product combines different elements into a unified whole. Some criteria: is it elegant, is it understandable, is it well crafted?

Writer's Mind
Editor's Mind
Creativity's dynamic balance

Great authors are of two minds. One is the writer's mind, the wildly imaginative, freewheeling renegade. The other is the editor's mind, which goes back after the writer's mind has done its work and weeds out the extraneous, non-value adding words, phrases and ideas. Not even the greatest writers can perform those two functions at the same time. In fact, the great writers are vigilant about keeping those two functions distinct.

The same principle applies to all creative thinking. Alex Osborn, in his breakthrough book *Applied Imagination*, noted two distinct kinds of thinking that are essential for being creative:

CREATIVITY ETIQUETTE RULE #1:

It is improper to diverge and converge at the same time.

Divergent thinking:
Generating lots of options, making lists

Convergent thinking:
Judging options, focusing, making decisions

We all do—and need to do—both kinds of thinking every day. The secret to creating new ideas is to become more conscious of which thinking mode you're in, so you can separate your divergent thinking from your convergent thinking.

When approaching a problem or challenge, first get into your writer's mind— your divergent mind—and generate lots of options. Only then should you put on your editor's critical thinking cap and begin to judge your ideas.

To Diverge...

Defer judgment
Strive for quantity
Seek wild ideas
Build on other
ideas

Ground Rules for Diverging

Why bother to generate lots of options? Research proves that more ideas produce better solutions. "Quantity yields quality," noted Alex Osborn, and Roger Firestien's 1987 research confirmed it: Those who used divergent thinking ground rules produced more than twice as many good ideas as those who didn't.

Defer Judgment.

Whatever idea comes to mind, go with it. Don't evaluate ideas while you are generating them. The ideas can be evaluated later.

Strive for quantity.

The more ideas you have, the greater the chances of getting a good one. Lay out all the usual approaches to the problem, then push to consider new options.

Seek wild and unusual ideas.

Freewheel—the wilder the ideas the better. Osborn said it's easier to tame a wild idea than to invigorate a weak one. Stretch your thinking to create some wild ideas.

Build on other ideas.

Let one idea spur other ideas. Build, combine and improve ideas.

Ground Rules for Converging

Converging involves judging and making decisions. Judging is a key part of creativity—and a delicate one. The wise judge chooses carefully and adheres to the following ground rules, to avoid dismissing fledgling ideas that might grow into robust and brilliant solutions. Remember, diverge first to generate lots of options. Then converge when it's time to make decisions.

Be affirmative.

Behind every creative act lies affirmative judgment. Even in convergence, it's important to discipline yourself to think "what's good about it?" before succumbing to the "no way !" reflex. Look for what you want, not just for what you don't want.

Be deliberate.

Avoid snap decisions or harsh judgments. Give every option a fair chance, and try to keep your own prejudices and assumptions in check.

Check your objectives.

Remember your original goal. Watch out for "sparkling" ideas that don't go in the right direction. In the face of too many good options, let your original objective be your guide.

Improve ideas.

Not all ideas are workable solutions. Even promising ideas must be honed and strengthened. Be disciplined. Take time to improve ideas.

Consider novelty.

Be brave. Don't dismiss original thinking out of hand. Consider ways to trim, tailor, or rework.

To Converge...

Be affirmative
Be deliberate
Check your objectives
Improve ideas
Consider novelty

In his book, Applied Imagination, *Alex Osborn proposed these rules for divergent thinking which are extremely effective in helping individuals and groups generate creative options. Scott Isaksen and Don Treffinger proposed similar rules for convergent thinking in* Creative Problem Solving: The Basic Course.

Traits* of Creative People

Sensitive
Not motivated by money
Sense of destiny
Adaptable
Tolerant of ambiguity
Observant
Perceive world differently
See possibilities others usually do not
Ask questions
Can synthesize and elaborate
Able to fantasize
Flexible
Fluent
Imaginative
Intuitive
Original
Ingenious
Energetic
Sense of humor
Self-actualizing
Self-disciplined
Self-knowledgeable
Specific interests
Divergent thinker
Curious
Open-ended
Independent
Severely critical
Non-conforming
Confident
Risk-taker
Persistent

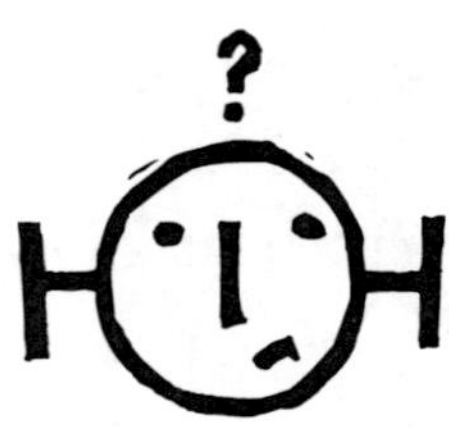

Not all traits apply to all creative people. Source: Robert Allen Black, Broken Crayons.

Tools for Diverging

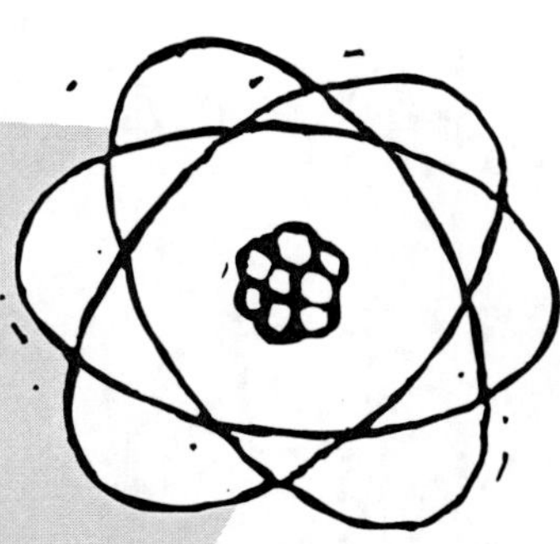

"Nothing is more dangerous than a new idea, when it's the only one you have."

EMILE CHARTIER

We become truly creative when we leave our assumptions and convictions behind and approach something with fresh eyes. We give up knowing and begin noticing. At this moment of "not knowing" creativity surfaces.

Divergent thinking is a way to articulate the known answers and push yourself—or a whole group—to the point of not knowing. The tools described in this section are fun to use. But, more importantly, they're critical for cracking open the door to creative thinking.

Brainstorming

Not just another bright idea

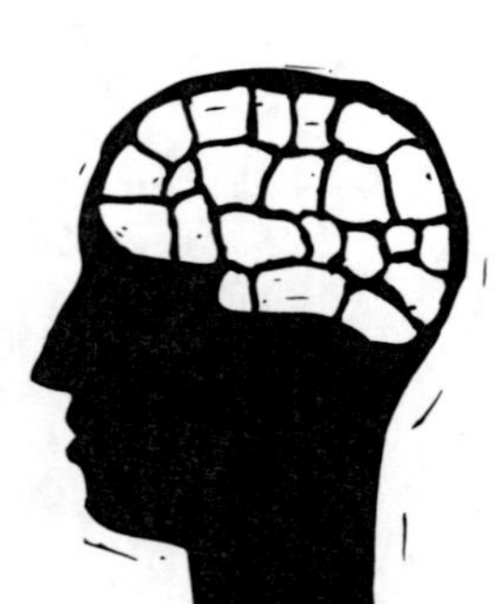

Remember the ground rules for divergent thinking!

- Defer judgment
- Strive for quantity
- Seek wild ideas
- Build on other ideas

Everyone's heard of brainstorming. But did you know that brainstorming was actually invented by Alex Osborn in 1953?

Osborn defined brainstorming as "a group's attempt to find solutions for a specific problem by amassing ideas." He did not define it as a bunch of people kicking around ideas and arguing about their relative merits.

Brainstorming is a pure form of divergent thinking. So as soon as you announce the problem to work on, BE SURE to review the ground rules for divergent thinking (at left).

Directions:

1.) Write the statement of the challenge you're working on so it's clearly visible.

2.) Review the ground rules for divergent thinking.

3.) Start thinking up options. Set a goal of at least 30 to 35. This quota seems high enough to purge the usual approaches to solving the problem and push you to consider new territory. Don't stop at the quota if you are really generating well.

4.) Record EVERY option in writing. If you're working with a group, have someone write on a flip chart. Be sure all the options are visible.

5.) Every 15 options or so, check to be sure you are still on track to meet the challenge.

6.) Keep going until you've met or exceeded your quota and have enough options to address the challenge.

Do you always need a group to brainstorm? Absolutely not. But keep in mind, even when you're by yourself, the four ground rules still apply!

Stick 'em Up Brainstorming

"Write a headline. Call it out!"

The 1980s brought the happy marriage between brainstorming and Post-it® notes, which led to the highly convenient, super speedy—and rather fun—technique of Stick 'em Up Brainstorming.

Directions:

1.) On a flip chart that's visible to all group members, write down the statement of the challenge you're working on.

2.) Review the ground rules for divergent thinking.

3.) Issue each participant a 3"x 5" pad of post-it notes and a dark, medium-tip magic marker.

4.) Set an idea quota and plan to push for new ideas until you meet it.

5.) Begin brainstorming on the challenge: If you have an idea, write it (in large print and in headline form) on a post-it note. Say your idea aloud and pass it forward to be posted on the flip chart.

6.) Every 15 ideas or so, check with the "owner" of the challenge to be sure the ideas are going in the right direction.

7.) Keep going until you meet your quota or have enough ideas to address the challenge.

Post-it note protocol:

• Write it down
• Say it out loud
• Hand it up

Brainstorming with Post-its is described by Scott Isaksen, Brian Dorval and Don Treffinger in Creative Approaches to Problem Solving.

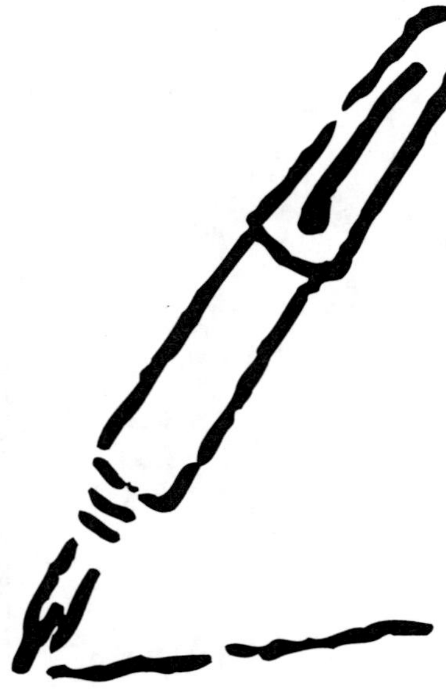

Brainwriting

"Write 3 and go!"

Another brainstorming technique is called "brainwriting." Developed by Horst Geschka, this modified form of brainstorming is an excellent way to give a group time to reflect on ideas and deliberately build on other thoughts. Because it is a more private, individualistic form of brainstorming, brainwriting is an excellent tool for dealing with groups where shy, quiet members are being overshadowed by more vocal ones. Surprisingly, even though brainwriting feels like a slower paced form of brainstorming, the actual number of ideas that results is often higher, because everyone in the group is working simultaneously.

Directions:

1.) Each person starts with a brainwriting worksheet (on opposite page).

2.) Put a blank worksheet in the center of the group.

3.) Write the statement of the challenge at the top of all worksheets.

4.) Review the ground rules for divergent thinking.

5.) Silently think of three ideas and write each one in a separate box on the first open row of your worksheet.

6.) Pass your worksheet back to the center and pick up one that someone else has just finished.

7.) Read the ideas on the new worksheet and build on them, or come up with three new ideas.

8.) Keep swapping worksheets until all the boxes are full. (Add more worksheets if necessary.)

Brainwriting Worksheet

29

Tools for Diverging

Forced Connections

What ideas do you get from this aardvark?

If you run out of ideas during a brainstorming session, try the Forced Connections technique. It works well with other divergent tools such as brainstorming and brainwriting. The unusual ideas that result often help get the group's mental wheels turning again.

Directions:

1.) Review the ground rules for diverging.

2.) Point to an object or picture totally unrelated to the problem and ask, "When you look at this (object or picture), what ideas do you get for solving this problem?"

3.) Force a connection between the item and the problem to generate more ideas. (Forced Connections often results in more novel or unusual options.)

4.) Share your ideas and repeat as necessary.

The Forced Connection question:

"When you look at this object or picture, what ideas do you get for solving this problem?"

Word Dance

Musical chairs with words

If all your efforts to restate the problem begin to sound the same, try Word Dance. It's a great tool for expanding the statement of the problem.

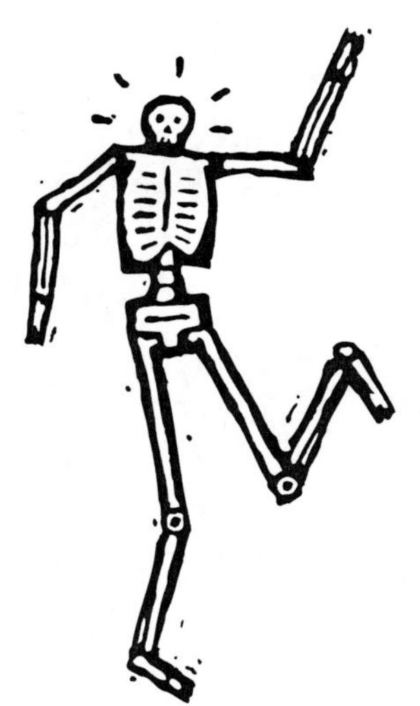

Directions:

1.) Start with your statement of the problem. Circle the verb and generate a series of verbs that could be used in its place.

2.) Now circle the "object" or "outcome" words. Again, generate a series of possible substitutes. Don't hesitate to be playful. Unusual choices often open promising new avenues.

3.) Mix and match, exploring various new combinations, and look for new insights into your problem.

4.) Choose the statement that expresses the problem in the most appealing and powerful way.

For example:

A social group wants to expand its membership. They have expressed their challenge as:

"How might we GET more MEMBERS?"

Playing Word Dance, they swap the verb "get" and the object "members" with a series of substitutes. They end up with similar challenges, with a new twist:

"How might we entice supporters?"
"How might we attract candidates?"
"How might we solicit more contributions?"

GET	MEMBERS
attract	participants
induce	supporters
solicit	leaders
entice	joiners
lure	candidates
gather	applicants
retain	registrations
collect	contributions
	groupies
	helpers

Tools for Diverging

SCAMPER

Divergent spark plug

Experience has shown that the best ideas are most often found among the last 33 percent of the ideas generated. That's why it's important to stretch people's thinking and generate lots of ideas. Alex Osborn, in his breakthrough book, Applied Imagination, *developed a series of questions that spark ideas during divergence. Bob Eberle categorized these questions in his book* Scamper: Games for Imagination Development, *and created the mnemonic SCAMPER to make them easier to remember.*

S ubstitute
C ombine
A dapt
M odify
P ut to other uses
E liminate
R earrange

(See next page for questions.)

SCAMPER Questions

To generate more ideas while brainstorming, ask the following questions in any order. Repeat the questions as necessary, but don't overwhelm yourself or the group by reading them in rapid succession. Take time to think and respond.

Substitute

What can you substitute?
What else can you use instead?
Who else can be included instead?
What other group can be included?
What other process can be used instead?
What other material can be used instead?

Combine

What can be combined?
How about a blend?
What sort of ensemble could be
used or created?
How can you combine parts?
How can you combine purposes?
How can you combine applications?
How can you combine materials?

Adapt

What other thoughts does this suggest?
What else is like this?
Does the past offer a similar situation?

Modify

How about a new twist?
How can you change the meaning?
How can you change the color or shape?
How about the sound?
What can you add?
How can you increase the height?
How can you increase the weight?

How can you add strength?
How can you increase frequency?
How can you increase value?
What can you subtract?
What can you shrink?
What can you streamline?
What can you understate?
How can you reduce the size?
How can you reduce the weight?

Put to other uses

What else can it be used for, as is?
What might other uses be, if changed?
What other markets might be interested?

Eliminate

What can you get rid of or omit?
What can you do without?
What can you sacrifice?
What can you give away?

Rearrange

What other patterns might work?
What other arrangements could be used?
What other layout might work?
What can you interchange?
What can you transpose?
What can you reconnect?
What if you reversed it?
What if you turned it upside down?
What if you turned it inside out?

Birthday checklist:
✔ Cake
✔ Gift
✔ Something personal
✔ Wear a suit

Combine for novelty.

The Idea Box
Combine key ingredients for novelty

The Idea Box is a great tool for generating lots of ideas in new and original combinations. Start by naming the essential characteristics of your challenge. Then build columns under each of those characteristics and fill them with relevant options. The fun starts when you begin combining options—one from each column—to discover original ideas.

Directions:

1. Pick the essential characteristics.
To create an Idea Box, start with your statement of the challenge, (e.g. How might I create a great story?) The challenge, then, is to create a story. What do you consider to be the essential characteristics of a story? You might decide: people, setting, timeframe and event are the essential characteristics you want to focus on.

2. Create column headings.
Take each characteristic you chose and put it at the top of a column.

3. Fill in options.
Under each characteristic, list a variety of options. For example:

People	Setting	Timeframe	Event
Doctor	Police Station	1950's	Win the Lottery
Journalist	Carnival	Renaissance	Lose job
Acrobats	Zoo	Ice Age	First date

4. Mix and match.
Now scan across the columns and combine options (one from each column) to come up with some new story ideas. You might choose: Journalist; Zoo; 1950's and First Date. What story ideas do these options give you?

5. Stretch beyond the literal.
In many cases, the literal combination won't be your end point. Stretch a step farther. For instance, zoo could be an animal park or a crazy environment, such as a daycare center, a World Cup Soccer Game, a bar on Friday night, etc.

Idea Box Worksheet

Statement of the challenge:

Write your statement of the challenge in the space above. Then, create column headings that describe the main characteristics or attributes of the challenge. Fill in each column with various options.

Tools for Diverging

Characteristics ☞

Options ☜

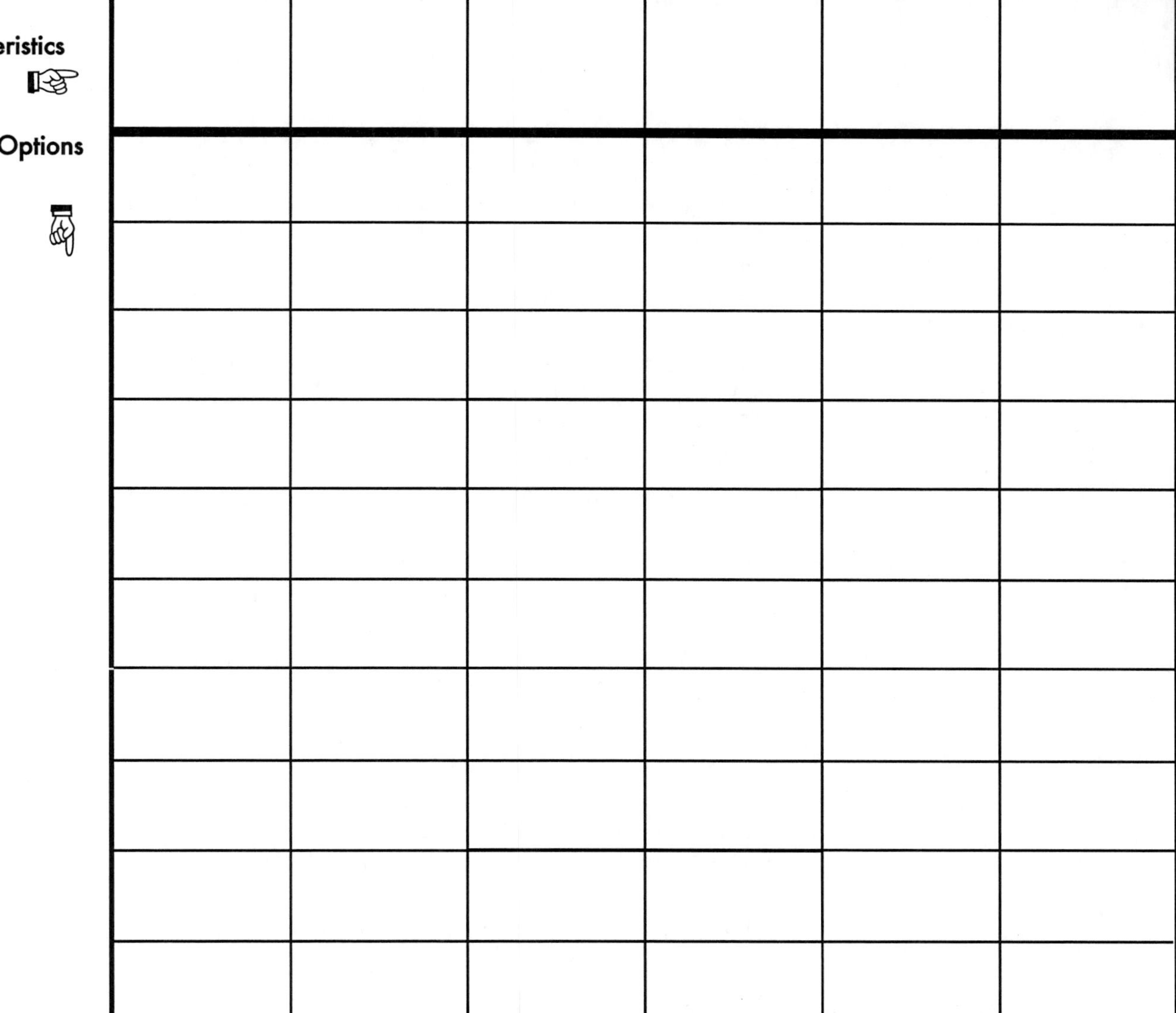

The Idea Box is based on the "Morphological Matrix." Read more in Discovery, Invention, Research through the Morphological Approach. *Zwicky, Fritz (1969). The Macmillan Company.*

Visual Connections

Going on a visual vacation

Sometimes, when you're in the middle of divergent thinking, it's helpful to change the cerebral scenery. Take a "tropical vacation." Visual connections is a divergent thinking tool that helps you relax, forget about the challenge you face, focus on an unrelated object for a while, and return to the action with fresh ideas. The results are often quite novel and unusual.

Directions:

1.) Collect a series of stunning or intriguing visuals to use as stimuli. Use toys, objects in the room or pictures. Pictures should not be readily identifiable (e.g. avoid photos of well known people, advertisements with text or logos).

2.) Take a moment to relax. Allow your mind to drift away from the challenge and float to your favorite vacation spot. Focus on what it looks like, smells like, sounds like and feels like. Notice the rich colors and beautiful weather.

3.) Come back and focus on the object. Write down any four observations, impressions, reactions or thoughts about the object. Remember, you're diverging. Don't edit yourself. Record your observations on the "Visual Connections Worksheet."

4.) Repeat step 3 with each visual stimulus.

5.) Write the statement of the challenge at the bottom of the "Visual Connections Worksheet."

6.) Take each of your observations and make a connection to the challenge. Record your connection on the form or on post-its (one connection per post-it) for a written record.

Visual Connections Worksheet

What do you see? What do you feel like? What would it be like if you were here? What memories have you had like this? What experiences have you had like this? What might this taste/sound/smell/feel like?

Object #1

Your observations from the stimulus

a)_______________________________

b) ______________________________

c)_______________________________

d) ______________________________

Connections to the challenge question

a) _______________________________

b) _______________________________

c)_______________________________

d) _______________________________

Object #2

Your observations from the stimulus

a)_______________________________

b) ______________________________

c)_______________________________

d) ______________________________

Connections to the challenge question

a) _______________________________

b) _______________________________

c)_______________________________

d) _______________________________

Object #3

Your observations from the stimulus

a)_______________________________

b) ______________________________

c)_______________________________

d) ______________________________

Connections to the challenge question

a) _______________________________

b) _______________________________

c)_______________________________

d) _______________________________

Statement of the challenge:

Visual Connections is derived from the work of W. Gordon (Synectics) and Horst Geschka (Methods and Organization of Idea Finding in Industry).

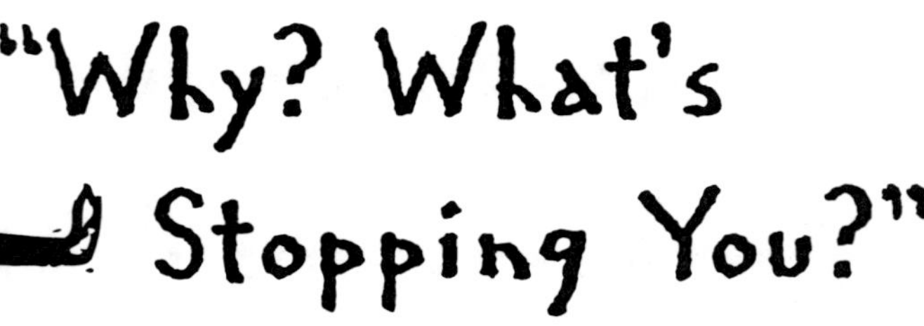

"Why? What's Stopping You?"

Isolate the right challenge to address

Brilliant solutions come from a thorough understanding of the problem area. Here is a simple tool to help someone get to the root of the problem.

It may look complicated at first, but it's really about asking two simple questions: Why? and What's stopping you? Then phrasing the answers as challenge questions using statement starters like "How to..." "How might..." "In what ways might..." or "What might be all the..."

Get at the REAL roadblock.

Directions:
Use this technique when you're trying to figure out the entire problem space.

"Why?"
1. First, write down your challenge question or goal / wish / challenge.
2. Ask "Why do you want to solve this challenge?" Listen closely.
3. Rephrase the answer as a challenge question, starting with "How to..." "How might..." etc. Write this down.
4. Take the new challenge question and replace "How to..." with "Why might you want to..." (For example, shift "How to increase profitability?" to "Why might you want to increase profitability?") Listen closely.
5. Rephrase the new response into a new challenge question starting with "How to..." "How might..." etc. Write this down.
6. Repeat steps 4-5 until you get to a statement such as "How to have a richer, fuller, life." At that point, don't bother asking why.

"What's stopping you?"
7. Now, return to the original statement and ask, "What's stopping you from solving this problem?" Listen closely.
8. Rephrase the answer as a challenge question beginning with "How to..." "How might..." etc. Write this down.

9. Take the new challenge question and replace "How to..." or "How might..." with "What's stopping you from..." (For example, shift "How to increase profitability?" to "What's stopping you from increasing profitability?") Listen closely.

10. Rephrase the response into a challenge question, starting with "How to..." "How might..." etc. Write this down.

11. Repeat steps 9 -10 until the challenge questions are so simple you no longer need to ask "What's stopping you?" (For example, "How might I find the number in the phone book?" At that point, you don't really need to ask, "What's stopping you?")

Ask.
Listen.
Rephrase.

Tools for Diverging

For example, start with the challenge question:
"How might I save money?"

Why?	**What's stopping you?**
You ask:	*Start again with the original challenge question:*
"Why might you want to save money?"	**"How might I save money?"**
You hear:	*You ask:*
"So I can take a vacation."	**"What's stopping you from saving money?"**
You rephrase as a challenge question:	*You hear:*
"How might I take a vacation?"	**"I don't make enough money."**
You ask:	*You rephrase as a challenge question:*
"Why might you want a vacation?"	**"How to make enough money?"**
You hear:	*You ask:*
"Because I want to spend time with my family."	**"What's stopping you from making enough money?"**
You rephrase as a challenge question:	*You hear:*
"How to spend more time with family?"	**"I need to take a certification course."**
You ask:	*You rephrase as a challenge question:*
"Why might you want to spend time with family?"	**"How to complete a certification course?"**
Keep asking "Why?" until the response is too broad, or too obvious to pursue, i.e.	*You ask:*
"Because it makes me happy."	**"What's stopping you from getting certified?"**
	Keep asking "What's stopping you" until you get a response that can be easily acted on:
then ask...	**"I need to register for the course."**

The Ladder of Abstraction used here was developed from the work of Sidney Parnes (The Magic of Your Mind), Scott Isaksen, Brian Dorval, and Don Treffinger (Creative Approaches to Problem Solving), and Min Basadur. The notion of extracting different levels of abstraction can be traced to the work of S.I. Hayakawa in 1978 which was based on the work of A. Korzybski in 1933.

OK, now I'll be the bathtub and you be the rubber duck.

Excursions

Let's blow this popstand...

An excursion is a creativity technique that takes people outside the context of their problem to look for inspiration in other—sometimes completely unrelated—areas. It's fun, and it works well to produce novel ideas. Excursions can include a variety of activities:

Visualization

To build a better beachball, take your group to Hawaii—in their minds. Dim the lights. Ask people to kick back in their chairs and shut their eyes. Paint a verbal picture, complete with the sights, sounds, smells, tastes and feelings of the island paradise. Aloha! Upon waking from this little reverie, ask the group what ideas they got from the trip. Build, stretch, imagine.

Role-Playing

To build a better bathtub, ask the group to act out taking a bath; play the part of the faucet or the tub; role-play a parent trying to get a toddler into a bath. Get ideas by springboarding off what the observers (or the role-players) notice.

"Field Trips"

Take an actual trip to the store, the zoo, the skating rink or the bus station. See what you can see. Be open to stimuli and ready to draw links to your own challenge.

Character Analogies

Tap into the minds of favorite teachers, famous inventors or even past presidents? Picture the person in your mind (i.e. Isaac Newton, Abraham Lincoln). Take a minute to think about his or her traits, personality and world view. Then generate ideas from that person's perspective.

Personal Analogies

Look at the challenge from the challenge's point of view. To build a better couch, imagine yourself to be a cushion. Generate ideas on the challenge from that perspective. Then change perspectives. Now you are one of the legs of the couch. What ideas does this perspective give you? It really works. Just ask Einstein! He solved many of his theoretical questions only after he imagined himself to be an actual beam of light.

Excursions Exercise

Ready, set, novelty!!!

Using excursions during sessions can be fun, challenging and highly effective. This may be a new experience for many people and using a warm-up is recommended. Excursions can be used individually or with groups.

Directions:

Every excursion will be unique, but you can use these guidelines:

- Review the ground rules for divergent thinking.
- Review the challenge statement and lead the group or yourself through the excursion.
- Generate ideas inspired by the excursion.
- Repeat if desired, using a different excursion.

"When I became a scientist, I would picture myself as a virus or cancer cell and try to imagine what it would be like."

Dr. Jonas Salk

Character Excursion for
"How might we grow our widget market share?"

Step 1: "Please close your eyes."
Step 2: "I'd like you to picture Abraham Lincoln." (Wait 15 to 30 seconds.)
Step 3: Think about some of Abraham Lincoln's traits—his personality, his perspective on the world. (Again give 45 seconds to think.)
Step 4: "Now turning to our challenge statement, what might be all the ideas that Abraham Lincoln would have for how we grow widget market share?"
Step 5: "Please record your ideas."
Initial ideas might include: give away samples along a train route; produce widgets with the Gettysburg address printed on them; hold an annual widget conference and invite dignitaries from around the world.
Step 6: Repeat from another perspective, say the Rolling Stones.

Personal Analogy Excursion for
"How to improve a bathtub?"

Step 1: Have the participants pretend they are the bathtub, the faucet or the bottom of the tub. "Imagine that you are the bottom of the tub. What do you feel? Want? Need?"(60 seconds)
Step 2: "From that perspective, what ideas do you have for how to improve a bathtub?"
Step 3: "Please record your ideas."
Initial ideas might include: a self-cleaning tub; a textured tub bottom; a tub that changes color as it gets dirty; a tub that read the mind of the person entering it and changes to their favorite color.
Step 4: Repeat, if desired from another perspective. For example, the showerhead.

Notes:

42

Tools for Converging

Critical judgment is essential for solving problems. The hazard comes in judging too soon—or choosing among options that are too limited.

In school, most of us got the clear message that the faster we got the answer, the smarter we were. In fact, the most successful problem solvers put in their time diverging before they enjoy the resolution that converging brings.

Tools for Converging

Highlighting

A quick way to screen options

Highlighting is a great way to take lots of ideas and narrow them to a few good options. This is a particularly effective tool when you want to clarify a problem or generate ideas. Highlighting helps you screen and select—to get the 80 percent value that's hidden in 20 percent of the options. In addition, highlighting helps make the remaining choices more manageable by grouping them into meaningful categories.

Remember: 80% of the value is hiding in 20% of the options.

Highlighting has three steps:
1.) Hits
2.) Cluster
3.) Restate

Hits
If you did a really ambitious job of diverging, you've ended up with more ideas than you can possibly use. That's good. Now, review all the ideas you've generated. Some will strike you as especially interesting, promising, compelling, intriguing, innovative or on-target. Mark or "hit" those ideas with a check, star or colored dot.

Cluster
After you mark your "hits," create groups or "clusters" of these related options to avoid duplication.

Restate
Look at your clusters. For each cluster, try to synthesize the different options into one statement. Resist the impulse to string all the ideas together into one long phrase or to edit them down into an oversimplified phrase. Instead, try to capture the essence and bring the cluster to life. A cluster of challenge questions will become a single challenge question. A cluster of ideas will become an elaborated idea. (See pages 46-47 for details.)

Characteristics of a "Hit"

on target	"sparkles"	solves the challenge
clear	intriguing	goes in the right direction
workable	interesting	"right on the money"
relevant	feels right	

Hits
mark the best ideas

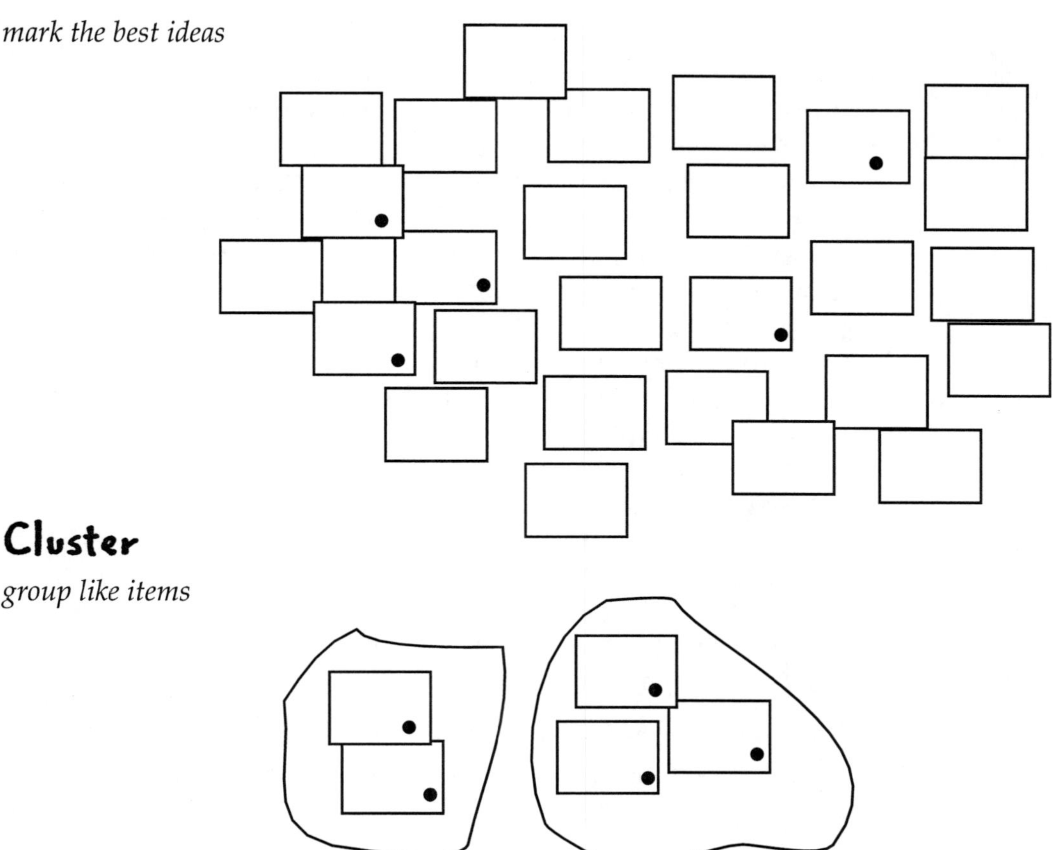

Cluster
group like items

Restate
bring the essence of the cluster to life

The characteristics of a "hit" were first presented by Roger Firestien and Donald Treffinger in
The Journal of Creative Behavior *(Vol. 17, no. 1, 1983).*

Tools for Converging

Restating Clusters

Solve the riddle
of the cluster
restatement and
the creative
breakthrough is
yours!

Once your most promising options, or hits, have been grouped together into clusters, it's time to restate the cluster. This is trickier than it looks. A brilliant restatement will dramatically increase your chances of creative breakthroughs. So spend time crafting this restatement. Don't just string the hits together or reduce them to the simplest common denominator. Chances are, you have grouped these options together because they are "getting at something." Your goal in restating the cluster is to articulate exactly what that "something" is and bring its essence to life. Synthesize. Find the synergy. Capture the kernel. This requires focus and determination, but the payoff is great.

For challenge questions

Use one of the following statement starters to restate the clusters…

How to... (H2)
In what ways might...(IWWM)
How might...(HM)
What might be all the...(WMBAT)

Hints: Be sure the challenge question is an open-ended question, not just an idea with a statement starter. Phrase it positively. Define the specific problem without getting bogged down by a lot of criteria.

Restating Challenge Questions

WATCH OUT for challenge questions that are actual ideas: *How might we introduce our new widget at the conference using our proven widget samples?*

BETTER. Use open-ended questions: *What might be all the ways we can introduce our new widget at the conference?*

WATCH OUT for challenge questions that are phrased negatively: *In what ways might we not lose widget market share?*

BETTER. Use positive phrasing: *How might we grow our widget market share?*

WATCH OUT for challenge questions that are too broad: *How to increase profit?*

BETTER. Define a specific problem: *How might we increase profit margins on widgets?*

WATCH OUT for challenge questions with too many criteria: *In what ways might we reduce inventory by 5000 units while staying responsive to sales people and maximizing our new sales projection process?*

BETTER. Keep free of criteria: *How might we reduce inventory?*

For Idea Clusters

Use the following statement starter to restate an idea cluster…
What we see ourselves doing is…(WWSODI)

Hints: For idea clusters, restatements can (and probably should) be much more than one sentence long. Think of the cluster as the skeleton and use as much space as you need to flesh out the ideas in it. Add details and include measurable and observable components.

Restating Idea Clusters

WATCH OUT. Avoid summarizing the idea cluster in one sentence. *What we see ourselves doing is reducing costs of producing widgets.*

BETTER. Elaborate on the ideas in the cluster, add details as well as measurable and observable components. *WWSODI reducing production costs by 25% in the next year by replacing our current production line with a new system capable of producing widgets of various sizes. We will also reduce our transportation costs by 15% in the next six months by switching to a new lighter packing material and renegotiating a long-term contract with our current delivery carrier. In addition, we will renegotiate our purchasing agreements to take ownership only upon delivery of acceptable inventory.*

WATCH OUT. Avoid oversimplifying the cluster. *WWSODI improving our internal communication.*

BETTER. Flesh out the ideas in the cluster and make the general, specific. *WWSODI breaking our current communication paradigm by developing a cross-functional team that includes 3 people each from marketing, finance, and research and development. This team will coordinate product development and marketing efforts to maximize our new product success rate. In addition, the team will meet once a week and develop an internal monthly newsletter that highlights new product success stories. The newsletter will be distributed and a website and email address will be set up to solicit questions, comments and ideas from employees worldwide.*

Tools for Converging

Behind every bright idea is a lot of careful thinking.

Praise First

Pluses, Opportunities, Issues, New thinking (POINt)

Most of us feel proud — and a little vulnerable — when presenting a new idea. Praise First is a four-step technique for evaluating and improving new ideas. Founded on the principle of affirmative judgment, Praise First allows you to express both positive and negative responses to an idea without crushing its potential—or its originator. When faced with a new idea, resist the inclination to point out its flaws. First, find the value in it. Express what you like about it. Second, say what opportunities might be possible if it worked. Only then should you present your issues. Phrase these issues as questions which invite new thinking. Finally, brainstorm to overcome any issues.

While Praise First is often associated with analyzing and improving ideas, you can also use it to give feedback on behaviors, projects or proposals. In fact, you might recognize it as the very same feedback method used by a favorite teacher, boss or grandparent. The four steps:

Pluses
What do you like about the person's idea, work, proposal or performance right now? Be direct, honest and specific.

Opportunities
What opportunities might this new idea open up? What might be potential spin-offs for future growth?

Issues
Express your concerns as open-ended questions that offer a possible direction for future development. Use the statement starters "How to...," "How might..." and "In what ways might...."

New thinking
Review your list of issues. Choose the most important and brainstorm to generate at least a dozen ways to overcome it. Do the same for the next most important issue on the list. Continue on until you overcome all your issues.

The PPC was originally developed in the early 1980s by Diane Foucar-Szocki, Bill Shephard and Roger Firestien.

Praise First Worksheet

If you have generated ideas and narrowed them down to a few promising options, here's your chance to strengthen, improve, and craft them into workable solutions. Begin by writing your most promising option(s) in the form of a "solution statement," beginning with the statement starter "What I see myself (us) doing is..." This statement should include a specific, measurable result. The measure can be as stringent as metrics or dollars, or as simple as verifying that you have accomplished the solution. Write your action statement below.

SOLUTION STATEMENT
What I see myself (us) doing is:

Tools for Converging

WAIT! Do not fill in the following chart until you have completed the next three pages.

In order to: **Do this:**

In order to: **Do this:**

In order to: **Do this:**

In order to: **Do this:**

In order to: **Do this:**

Praise First

Now, run a Praise First or POINt on your solution statement. Remember, POINt stands for Pluses, Opportunities, Issues and New thinking. The idea is to articulate what's good about the idea, then to consider and overcome any issues you have.

Below list at least three **pluses** or specific strengths of your solution.

1.

2.

3.

Now, list at least three **opportunities**, speculations, spin-offs or possible future gains that could result from your solution. "In a future when this solution has become a reality, what has become possible?" List opportunities, using the statement starter "It might..."

1. *It might:*

2. *It might:*

3. *It might:*

Finally, list any **issues** you have with the idea. Be sure to phrase your issues as open-ended questions that will allow you to overcome each one and move forward.

1. *How to:*

2. *How to:*

3. *How to:*

Review your issues. Decide which are most important. List your most important issue below and generate at least 15 ideas to overcome it. Once you have enough **new thinking** to overcome that issue, go to your next most important issue and generate ideas to overcome it. Do this until you have new thinking that helps overcome each issue. Remember, use the ground rules for diverging when you stretch for new thinking to overcome your issues.

Issue #1) How to...
New thinking for overcoming issue #1:

1.	9.
2.	10.
3.	11.
4.	12.
5.	13.
6.	14.
7.	15.
8.	

Issue #2) How to...
New thinking for overcoming issue #2:

1.	9.
2.	10.
3.	11.
4.	12.
5.	13.
6.	14.
7.	15.
8.	

Issue #3) How to...
New thinking for overcoming issue #3:

1.	9.
2.	10.
3.	11.
4.	12.
5.	13.
6.	14.
7.	15.
8.	

Tools for Converging

Issue #4) How to...

New thinking for overcoming issue #4:

1.
2.
3.
4.
5.
6.
7.
8.

9.
10.
11.
12.
13.
14.
15.

Issue #5) How to...

New thinking for overcoming issue #5:

1.
2.
3.
4.
5.
6.
7.
8.

9.
10.
11.
12.
13.
14.
15.

Put check marks by the best ideas for overcoming each issue.

NOW, turn back to page 49 and fill in the rest of the chart. Take each issue and rewrite it using the statement starter "In order to..." Then include your best ideas for overcoming each issue in the space labeled "Do this."

For example, an issue over funding might start as:
"How might I get funding?"

After brainstorming, you might end up filling in page 49 by writing:
"In order to obtain funding, we will petition the division vice president and prove a cost-reduction over the next 18 months."

PPC is a creativity tool developed by Multiple Resource Associates.

Card Sort

Ranking the options

Card sort is a convergent tool that helps you compare, rank and prioritize promising options. It can be used to rank ideas, solutions, challenge questions or criteria. Card Sort also helps to generate group consensus. Use it to help prioritize up to 15 options.

Materials:

3"x 5" cards (or scraps of paper)

Directions:

1. Write each option down on a separate card and arrange the cards before you in a row.

2. Count how many cards (options) you have.

3. Identify the option you like the least. On that card write the number that equals the total number of cards you have. For example, if you have five option cards, write "5" on your least favorite option. Put this card off to the side.

4. Of the cards remaining, identify the option you like best and write "1" on it. Put it off to the side.

5. Of the cards remaining, identify the option you like least. On it, write the second highest number (total cards minus one). Put it off to the side.

6. Of the remaining options, identify the one you like best. Write "2" on it, and put it off to the side.

7. Continue this process until all the cards have been removed.

8. Arrange the cards in numerical order. You now have a prioritized list of options.

Tools for Converging

Evaluation Matrix
Seeing how the options stack up

The evaluation matrix is a convergent tool that creates a systematic way to analyze up to 10 options. It's a good tool for building consensus because it allows a group to select criteria and evaluate a variety of promising options against the criteria they selected.

Directions:

1. Generate Criteria
To create an evaluation matrix, first decide on the criteria you want to use to judge your options. To generate criteria, ask yourself, "What does my idea have to be for me to want to do it?" For example, when buying a new home, you may consider some of the criteria to be: initial cost of home, cost of upkeep, location, access to public transportation, school district, taxes etc. Phrase the criteria as questions, using the statement starters "Will it..." "Does it..."or "Is it..." (i.e. Is it near public transportation? Does it cost less than $200,000? Does it require less than $3,000 in renovations?) Be sure to phrase the questions to get positive responses. For example, if you want to spend less than $100 on something ask, "Will it cost less than $100?" not "Will it be more than $100?" (This will be important later, when you rate the options.)

2. Select criteria
Choose the criteria most important or influential for your decision. The more specific the criteria, the more valuable the matrix. Any measurements you can include will strengthen the evaluation.

3. Begin to set up the matrix
Write your chosen criteria along the top of the matrix, forming a column for each. Then, list your options down the left side of the matrix. Create a rating scale. (You can use A, B, C, D, E, F, in the sense of a traditional grading scale, or any other scale you feel comfortable using.)

4. Fill in the blank boxes
Using your rating scale, fill in the boxes one column at a time. This way, you systematically judge each option against the same criteria. To help you rate, ask yourself: "If (option), to what extent (criteria)?" For example: "If we buy a house on Main Street, to what extent will it be near the bus lines?"

5. Complete the matrix.

Finish filling in the boxes, but don't total up the rows. The matrix is not intended to score options, but to let you compare their strengths and weaknesses. Seeing the different ratings can help clarify your thinking. Look at the options that got high and low ratings. Factor those ratings into your decision-making process.

6. Overcome low criteria ratings.

If necessary, diverge on ideas for how to overcome low ratings.

Evaluation Matrix Worksheet

Rating scale: Excellent   Okay   Poor
A   B   C   D   E

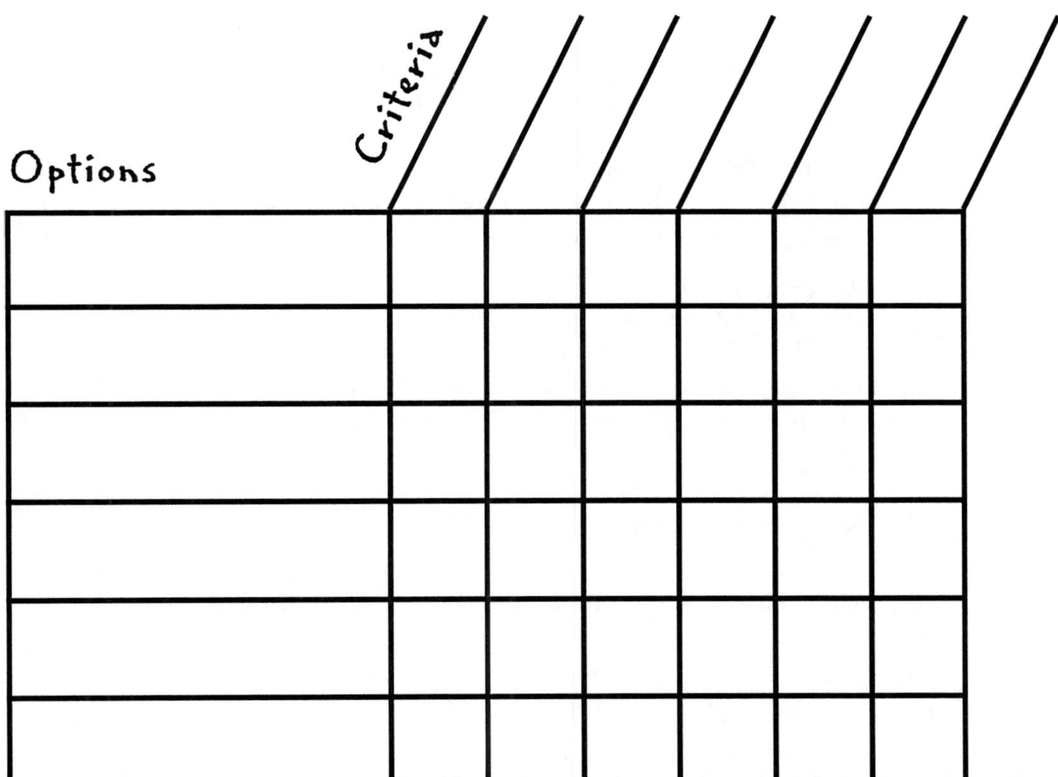

Sidney Parnes uses the evaluation matrix in his Creative Behavior Guidebook and Creative Behavior Workbook.

Tools for Converging

Targeting
Approaching the ideal solution

Targeting is a highly visual approach to evaluating and strengthening options. It is a flexible, effective tool that helps groups cut through tension and adversarial debate to surface areas of agreement and opportunities for building consensus. Targeting is designed to be intuitive, visual and interactive, letting you compare your current options to an ideal outcome and giving you an instant read on the gap between the ideal and the real.

Directions:

1. Define the bull's-eye: To start, define and articulate your ideal state. Generate all the attributes of your ideal state and place them in the center of the target. This is your bull's-eye.

2. Throw your darts: Write each option on a sticky note. Place this "dart" on the target in relationship to how close this option comes to meeting the ideal state. For instance, if you feel an option directly meets the qualities of the ideal state, put your dart in the bull's-eye. If it doesn't quite fit, locate the dart on one of the outer rings.

3. Identify Pulls & Pushes: Once the darts are on the target, identify those forces pulling the idea towards the bull's-eye and those forces pushing the option away from the bull's-eye. Pushes and pulls can be people, processes, systems, attitudes or other factors.

4. Turn pushes into challenge statements: Identify the most important pushes on your list. Transform these pushes into challenge statements by using one of the following statement starters, "How to? How might? In what ways might? What might be all the?"

5. Overcome challenges: Start brainstorming on the most significant challenge. When you have enough ideas, look back at the target. Have these ideas helped move the dart closer to the bull's-eye? Continue to overcome challenges until the dart has moved to the bull's-eye.

6. Ready, set, go! Use the ideas generated to overcome challenges to strengthen your solution statement by rewriting your solution statement using the phrase, "What I NOW see myself doing is…"

Targeting was developed by Blair Miller and Gerard Puccio of the International Center for Studies in Creativity.

Targeting worksheet

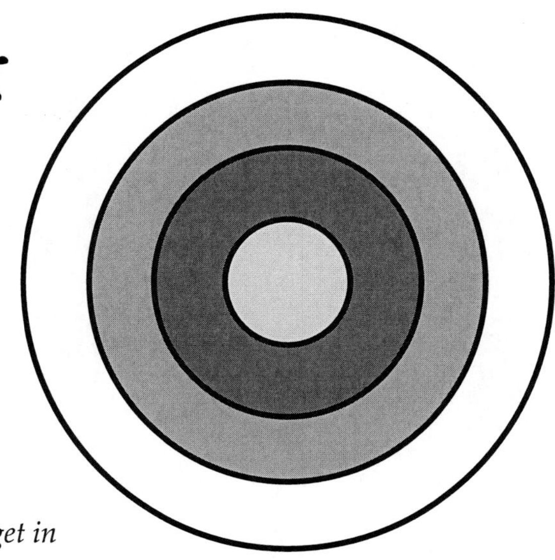

The bull's-eye:
In the space below, describe your ideal state: Use pictures, words, and other visuals to bring your ideal state to life.

Where are you now?
Place the dart (option; what I see myself doing is…) on the target in relation to your ideal state.

Why are you off center?
Explain the forces that pull the idea toward the center (i.e. why it's good) and the forces that push it away (why it's not exactly on target).

Pulls   Pushes

What would help get you to the bull's-eye?
Turn pushes into "How to…" statements and brainstorm ideas.

How to…   Ideas:

How to…   Ideas:

How to…   Ideas:

Ready, Set, Go!
Pick the ideas that will help turn pushes into pulls and write a new action statement using the statement starter…What I now see myself doing is…

TERMS

Bull's-eye: Your ideal/future state
Dart: The best option(s) you are considering
Pull: Positive force that pulls the option towards the bull's-eye
Push: Negative force that pushes the option away from the bulls-eye

Notes:

What is Creative Problem Solving?

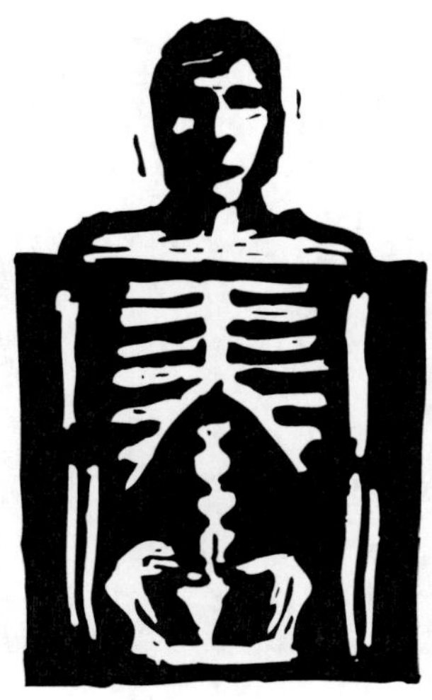

"...problem solving and creative thinking are closely related. The very definitions of those two activities show logical connections. Creative thinking produces novel outcomes, and problem solving involves producing a new response to a new situation, which is a novel outcome."

J.P. GUILFORD (1977)

Everyone solves problems, in the same way that everyone has music in their soul. But people who take music lessons and practice tend to play better.

CPS gets to the bones of the creative process.

What is CPS?

The Mother of Invention

CPS as an intuitive process

A few years back, a renowned inventor—with a record number of patents for an international computer company—decided to analyze the exact steps he took to come up with his breakthrough innovations. He started attending courses on creativity and promptly stumbled into a course on Creative Problem Solving. After the five-day course, he realized he'd have to redirect his efforts. He told one of the trainers that he no longer needed to record his creative process, tools and techniques. Creative Problem Solving had already done it.

One reason Creative Problem Solving is so effective is because, for the most part, it simply describes a natural process. Everybody solves problems. And everybody uses roughly the same process to do it. Making the whole process explicit lets everyone know where they are, and where they're going. People don't get lost in the problem. And the solutions—because they result from carefully crafted creativity techniques and group input—are often innovative and right on target.

Roles in a CPS Session

When using CPS in a group, there are distinct roles to assign.

Facilitator

The facilitator is the Creative Problem Solving "process expert"—the person (or team of people) responsible for keeping track of logistics, idea flow and group development. Generally, facilitators do not contribute ideas or help converge on ideas. Instead, they focus on making CPS process decisions, based on the client's input. They also meet with the client before convening the resource group.

Client

The client—who can be an individual or a group—is the primary "owner" of the challenge being explored. The client lets the facilitator worry about CPS process and focuses instead on the data and decision making around the challenge itself. The client is responsible for sharing background information, generating ideas along with the resource group, providing direction for the facilitator and selecting ideas that best address the challenge. (Note: the client is generally the only one who gets to diverge *and* converge.)

Resource Group

The resource group provides ideas, energy, insight and dynamic perspectives for the CPS session. They take direction from the facilitator and diverge like crazy to serve the client.

Alex Osborn first addressed the roles and responsibility of the facilitator in his book Applied Imagination *(1953). Subsequently, the role of the resource group was explained by Donald Treffinger and Roger Firestien in the* Journal of Creative Behavior *and the role of the client was defined by Donald Treffinger, Scott Isaksen and Roger Firestien in the* Handbook of Creative Learning.

The "Ownership" Issue

There's nothing worse than trying to solve a problem that isn't yours. It can be a time-wasting and frustrating exercise. That's why ownership is so important as a criteria to determine if CPS is the right approach.

Ownership means being accountable for the solution to the problem. You "own" the problem if it's your problem to solve and you've got agreement with others that you're accountable.

Questions to test for ownership:

- *Is this your problem to solve?*
- *Are others counting on you to implement a solution to this problem?*
- *Are you willing to be held accountable for accomplishing this goal (and suffer the consequences if you don't)?*

If the answer to the above questions is "yes," then proceed—with caution. You've still got two other criteria to apply before you can be sure that CPS is the right approach to your challenge. Here are all three criteria. Remember them by the acronym "OMI."

1. Ownership	**2. Motivation**	**3. Imagination**
It's your problem to solve. You have influence and accountability.	*You really want to take action.*	*The problem really requires novelty or new thinking.*

Got all three? What are you waiting for? You've got problems to solve and opportunities to find!

William Shephard and his associates at Multiple Resource Associates (MRA) began working with ownership issues and CPS in the early '80s. The results of this work were published in 1983 by Roger Firestien (also of MRA) and Donald Treffinger and by Scott Isaksen.

Statement Starters

IW, IWBGI, H2, ...hmmm

Creative Problem Solving relies on word power to encourage affirmative judgment and frame problems in their most approachable light.

Statement starters are the clearest example of CPS word power. They are set phrases, used to begin statements of ideas or problems. The phrasing is designed to focus the brain on generating options and considering solutions, rather than shutting down ideas and blocking possibilities.

For example, it's natural to voice a concern about cost by saying, "It's too expensive." But such phrasing is likely to cut off discussion or spark an argument. If, instead, you used the statement starter "How might...," you naturally invite ideas for overcoming the concern. For example, "How might we make it less expensive?" Or, "How might we obtain funding from other sources."

When expressing concerns, use the statement starters: There's a statement starter associated with several (but not all) of the stages in CPS.

Clarify

The vision:
It would be great if... (IWBGI)
I wish... (IW)

The challenge:
How to... (H2)
How might... (HM)
In what ways might... (IWWM)
What might be all the... (WMBAT)

Develop

The solution:
What I see myself (us) doing is... (WISMDI)
What I NOW see myself (us) doing is...(WINSMDI)
When generating criteria, use *Will it..., Does it..., Is it...*

What your English teacher would say:

Statement Starter + Noun + Verb + Object.

*Example: **How might + we + get + funding** for this project?*

FourSight® Model

CPS in a nutshell

The steps of the CPS process may feel familiar, logical, even obvious. They should. Remember, they are descriptive of how we all work through problems and challenges.

Over the years, CPS has been represented by dozens of different models. Some have six steps, some seven, some four. They're all good. Even Alex Osborn, the originator of CPS, proposed a variety of models over his lifetime.

Our job is to start you off with a working model that gets you up and problem solving in no time. The FourSight model is our favorite. There are four basic steps: clarify, ideate, develop and implement.

FourSight model developed by Dorte Nielsen and Sarah Thurber (2010), based on the work of Gerard Puccio and Blair Miller (2003). Used with permission.

Creative Heartbeat
Diverge and converge make the pulse

Everybody solves problems. But not everybody solves them creatively.

The big difference...
The secret from moving from "problem solving" to "*creative* problem solving" is deliberately separating the divergent and convergent part of *each* step of the process.

So when you clarify, think of lots of data before you select the key data. Think of lots of ways to frame the problem before you choose your breakthrough question. When you ideate, think of lots (and lots) of ideas before converging on your top choices. Even develop and implement call for diverging and converging. That's why the model is composed of diamonds — to remind you to diverge and converge at each step.

Why bother?
Research shows that you get better, richer, more effective solutions when you create more options.

If you move through each step only considering the obvious solutions, you're less likely to get a breakthrough. Diverging forces you outside of your comfort zone. It encourages you to push beyond the obvious. That's where innovation awaits.

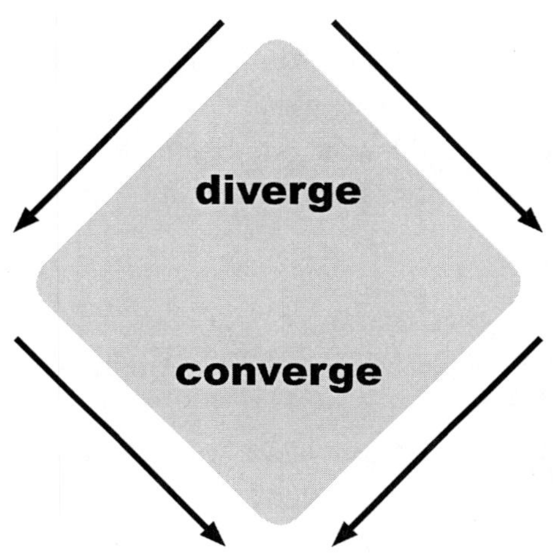

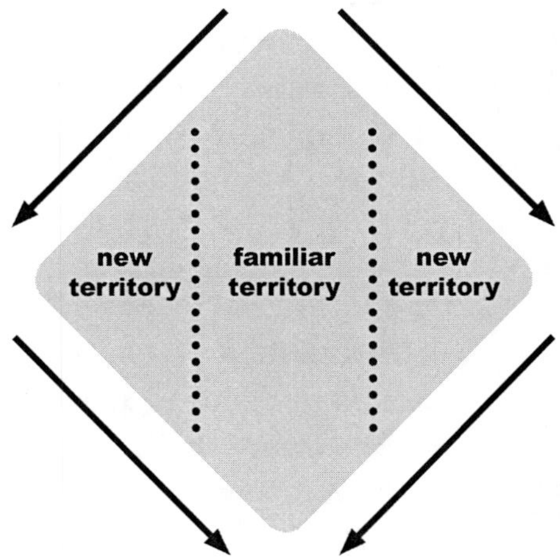

What is CPS?

Essential CPS
The four basic steps

Clarify

Goal: To understand the challenge at hand. (What's the goal? What's the key information? What's the problem you're trying to solve?)
Start here when: You have a goal in mind.
Finish with: An open-ended question that invites new ideas about the challenge.

Ideate

Goal: To explore *lots* of ideas to help you address your challenge
Start here when: You need novel, useful ideas to meet your challenge.
Finish with: Selected ideas to help solve the challenge.

Develop

Goal: To turn promising ideas into workable solutions
Start here when: You have some good ideas that need strengthening.
Finish with: A well developed, detailed solution.

Implement

Goal: To put your idea into action
Start here when: You have a strong solution that's ready for action.
Finish with: An action plan that shows how to test and sell your solution.

Assess the Situation
The power of a proper diagnosis

While the process may look linear — like an A-Z affair — it's not. It's far more flexible than that. Where you begin depends on what you need to work on. And the steps don't always flow in order. Sometimes you start developing a solution only to find out you need more clarification. Sometimes you implement a plan and realize you need to back up and develop the solution a bit more.

Doctor CPS

Begin with a diagnosis. Start by gathering data and assessing where you need to enter the process. You might even decide that CPS isn't the right approach.

That kind of sensitivity to the challenge grows over time. Just remember that the process is flexible and the starting point is always to "assess."

Data Questions

Here are some questions you can ask. Remember that "data" can consist of facts, emotions, group perceptions or intuitions.

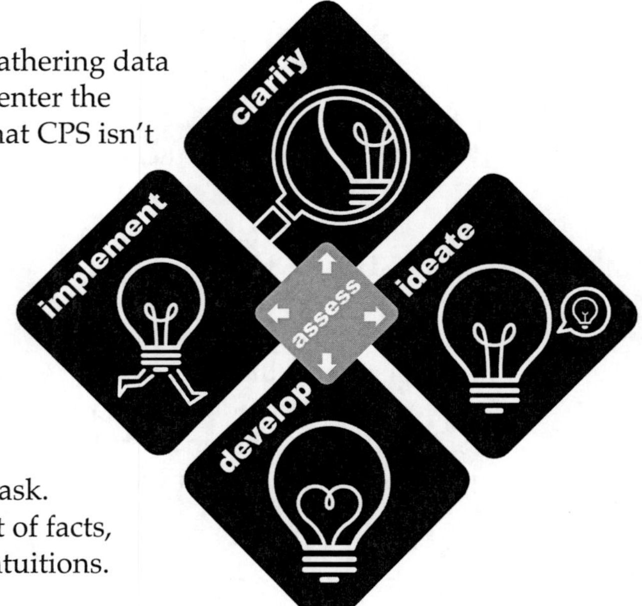

- What is a brief history of the situation?
- Who is involved?
- Who is the decision maker?
- How do you own this situation?
- Who might gain if the situation is resolved?
- What successes have been achieved so far?
- What has promoted those successes?
- What are some of the obstacles you encountered?
- Where have you found help?
- When does this situation seem to occur?
- When would you like to see action taken on this situation?
- How long has it been a concern?
- Why is this a concern or opportunity for you?
- What have you already thought of or tried?
- What are the needs of the end user?

Clarify

Get clear on the challenge

Start here when...
You want to identify the goal or desired outcome of your efforts. You need to pinpoint the right challenge or opportunity to pursue.

Explore the Vision
Here's your chance to generate a whole list of "wish statements" and choose the one that best fits your goal. Begin each item on the list with a statement starter like:

"I wish..."
"It would be great if..."

Pick one and write it in the clarify worksheet on the next page under the heading "What's next?"

Formulate the Challenge
After listing all the data relevant to your goal, wish or challenge, start diverging on possible ways to approach it. Remember to phrase challenges as questions, and don't stop at one. Begin each item on the list with a statement starter like:

"How to..."
"How might..."
"In what ways might..."
"What might be all the..."

Write 10 possible approaches to the challenge and then put a check by your "challenge question."

"There are an infinite number of solutions. Now which question were you asking?"

ALBERT EINSTEIN

CLARIFIER mind set	Tool set
Clarifiers are strategic thinkers. They identify gaps. They see opportunities. They fuel their thinking with facts and information. They keep clarifying until they really understand the right challenge to address.	• Gather Data Questions • Phrase challenges as open-ended questions • Word Dance • Why? What's stopping you?

Clarify Worksheet

What's next?
Where do you need a breakthrough?
I wish...
It would be great if...

Data dump: What's a brief summary of your situation?
Write the facts, history, key players, big opportunities,
current intuitions & criteria for success.

The challenge question...
Reread your goal. Review the data. Now your job is to pinpoint the challenge that, if met, will help
you achieve a breakthrough. Look at your data and begin to formulate open-ended questions.
Don't stop at one or two. Find a question that breaks open the problem and invites solutions.

Begin each question a phrase like...

1. *How to...*

2. *How might...*

3. *In what ways might...*

4. *What might be all the...*

5.

6.

7.

8.

9.

10.

Check marks the breakthrough. Put a ✔ mark by the question that you believe points you in
the direction of a breakthrough. Write it at the top of the next page.

What is CPS?

Ideate

Generate lots of ideas

Start here when...
You have a clearly defined challenge and you need ideas to solve it.

Explore Ideas

Now that you've got the "challenge question," start exploring possibilities, ideas and options that might work. Start with the obvious and then go wide.

Follow the divergent guidelines

More than ever, this is a time to defer judgment, strive for quantity, seek wild and unusual ideas, and build on other ideas. Bump your brain out of its comfort zone and consider novel approaches. Look at silly and ridiculous ideas. No need to commit. You're just diverging here.

Idea shop

Once you've got a big pool of ideas to choose from, pick your favorites. See if they cluster into natural groupings of ideas that express the same or very similar ideas. These will be the ideas you carry forward into the next step.

IDEATOR mind set	Tool set
Ideators are imaginative thinkers. They grasp the big picture. They can mix and match ideas to create new possibilities. They fuel their thinking with play and variety. They keep ideating until they've come up with something truly original and "spot on."	• Brainstorming • Brainwriting • Forced Connections • Idea Box •Visual Connections • Excursions

"The best way to get good ideas is to have lots of ideas."

LINUS PAULING
NOBEL PRIZE WINNER

Ideate Worksheet

Rewrite your "challenge question" here:

Diverge:
Generate as many ideas as you can for solving the challenge. Remember that quantity yields quality. Your first 5-7 ideas might be obvious. Your next 5-7 might be a bit harder. Stay with it. The last third is where some of the best new thinking emerges. Stuck? Try brainstorming with others!

1	16
2	17
3	18
4	19
5	20
6	21
7	22
8	23
9	24
10	25
11	26
12	27
13	28
14	29
15	30

Idea shop:
Converge! Review your list of ideas. Put a ✔ mark by the most interesting and promising. These are the ideas you'll carry forward into the next stage.

My breakthrough (so far):
Incorporate all your chosen ideas into an initial breakthrough solution. Write it in paragraph form on the next page. Rather than use bullet points, write a vivid description, full of details. Think of it more like a journal entry than a check list. Include specific activities, measurements and times, so even a stranger could read your solution and fully understand what you intend to do.

'God is in the details."

MIES VAN DER ROHE

Develop
Select and strengthen solutions

Start here when...
You want to turn promising ideas into workable solutions.

Formulate solutions
Here's where you sift through your high-potential possibilities and pick the "jewel of an idea" that you're willing to spend time refining, polishing and honing into a brilliant solution.

Dear Diary...
Begin by reviewing your top ideas and synthesizing them into a "story" of what you're planning to do next. Write it almost like a journal entry, giving rich details, clear deadlines and measurable results. Begin with the statement starter:

"What I see myself doing is..."

Get to the POINt evaluation
Now review your narrative description (a.k.a. your "solution statement") and consider, what are its pluses? What opportunities might it provide in the future? What issues might need to be addressed? Can you offer new thinking to overcome those issues?

Once again, review your solution statement and this time, add to it. Based on what you learned from the POINt evaluation you just did, how might you improve it?

DEVELOPER mind set	Tool set
Developers are evaluative thinkers. Their gift is selecting, improving and refining ideas. They fuel their thinking with attending to the finer details of how a solution will work in context. They value a well thought out solution.	• POINt • Evaluation matrix • Card sort • Targeting

Develop Worksheet

My solution statement:
What I see myself doing is…

____

____

____

____

____

____

____

____

Improve your solution with a POINt evaluation:

What are its Pluses?

Opportunities?

Issues?

What New thinking might be necessary?

After your POINt evaluation, strengthen your solution by incorporating your new thinking.
To strengthen my solution, I'll also…

What is CPS?

"Often the difference between a successful man and a failure is not one's better abilities or ideas, but the courage that one has to bet on his ideas, to take a calculated risk — and to act.

MAXWELL MALTZ

Implement
Put the plan into action

Start here when...
You need buy-in from others and an action plan to follow.

Explore acceptance
Here's where the rubber meets the road. You've got a well thought-out solution, and you're ready for action. But is everyone else? Time to be sure you've got buy-in from those that can make or break the success of this solution.

Make a list of who or what can assist you. Write down how you might enlist their help. Make a list of potential "resisters" (people or things that will resist your solution) and how you might overcome their resistance. Select those that will be your critical area of focus.

Formulate a plan
Finally, it's time to write the "to do" list. Write down everything you can think of. Then choose the key steps that will move your solution to success. Sort them into short-term, mid-term and long-term activities. Commit to do something in the next 24 hours to build momentum.

Learn on your feet
Learn from your successes and failures. Ask "debriefing questions" like: What worked? What didn't? What will you do again differently next time?

IMPLEMENTER mind set	Tool set
Implementers are tactical thinkers. They are practical and savvy and not averse to a little risk. They fuel their thinking by testing, prototyping, trying things out to see what works. They value the courage to take action.	• Assister / Resisters • Action Plan • Debriefing questions

Implement Worksheet

My action plan!
Read over your solution statement on the "develop" page.

Consider:
What steps might help put my breakthrough into action?
What resources might help (people, materials, money, location, etc.)
What obstacles can I anticipate?
How might I test the solution?

Incorporate these ideas into the to-do list below.
Write who will do what by when.
Indicate who needs to know when the job is complete.

To do...	Who	By when?	Report to...
Short term			
1.			
2.			
3.			
Mid term			
1.			
2.			
3.			
Long term			
1.			
2.			

In the next 24 hours, I will...

Take responsibility for your thinking. Be the breakthrough you want to create!

What is CPS?

Process Overview

Process step	Start here when	Statement starters
Assess Gather data Diagnose	You want to figure out where to begin in the CPS process.	Who? What? When? Where? Why? How?
Clarify Explore the vision Formulate challenges	You want to set a goal or desired outcome. You want to pinpoint the challenge to address.	I wish... It would be great if... How to... How might... What might be all the...?
Ideate Explore ideas	You want novel, useful ideas to address your challenge.	
Develop Formulate solutions	You want to turn promising ideas into workable solutions.	What I see myself doing is... Criteria: Is it...? Will it...? Does it...?
Implement Explore acceptance Formulate a plan	You want the environment to support your thinking. You want to implement your solution.	

Mind set	Tool set	Outcome
When you assess, ask "where in the process should I start working on this challenge?"	Gather data questions	A clear picture of where to be and where to go in the CPS process
Clarifiers are strategic thinkers. They identify gaps. They see opportunities. They value facts and information.	• Gather data questions • Phrase challenges as questions • Why? What's stopping you?	A statement of the goal, wish or challenge A well-defined challenge question
Ideators are imaginative thinkers. They get the big picture. They mix and match ideas to create new possibilities.	• Brainstorming • Brainwriting • Forced Connections • Visual Connections • Excursions	One or more ideas that will solve the challenge
Developers are evaluative thinkers. They select, improve and refine ideas to get the solution "just right" for its context.	• POINt • Evaluation matrix • Card sort • Targeting	Well developed, detailed and improved solutions
Implementers are tactical thinkers. They learn by testing and prototyping to see what works.	• Assisters/Resisters • Action Plan • Debriefing questions	A plan for taking action

Notes:

Creativity Resources

Creativity Articles

Real World CPS Successes

CPS References

The Value of Clarifying the Problem

A Seafaring Example

From Thinkertoys *by Michael Michalko*

They were doing
things right, but
they weren't
doing the right
thing.

In the 1950s, experts believed that the ocean-going freighter was dying. Costs were rising, and it took longer and longer to get merchandise delivered. The longer goods piled up waiting to be loaded, the more theft happened at the docks.

The shipping industry formulated their challenge as: "In what ways might we make ships more economical at sea and while in transit from one port to another?"

They built ships that were faster or required less fuel, and reduced crew size. Costs still kept going up, but the industry kept concentrating its efforts on reducing the specific costs related to ships while at sea and doing work. They were doing things right, but they weren't doing the right thing.

A ship is capital equipment and the biggest cost for the capital equipment is the cost of not working. Finally, a consultant stretched the industry's challenge to: "In what ways might the shipping industry reduce costs?"

This allowed them to consider all aspects of shipping, including loading and stowing. The innovation that saved an industry was to separate loading from stowing, by doing the loading on land, before the ship is in port. It is much quicker to take on and take off preloaded freight. They decided to concentrate on the costs of not working rather than working, and reduce the amount of time a freighter does not work. The answer was the roll-on, roll-off ship and the container ship.

This simple solution was the direct result of reframing the challenge. The results have been startling. Freighter traffic has increased fivefold in the last 30 years, and costs are down by 60 percent. Port time has been reduced by 75 percent, and congestion and theft has declined. ✳

From Thinkertoys *by Michael Michalko, Ten Speed Press, Berkeley, California 1991*

The Importance of Making Mistakes

One of the IBM corporation's legends is an incident that occurred in its very early years. It seems that IBM's founder, Thomas Watson, Sr. had a manager that lost 10 million dollars for the company in a failed venture. The man thought that the only honorable thing to do was to commit organizational suicide. He prepared his resignation and went in to see Mr. Watson.

The employee handed his resignation to Watson. Watson looked at the man, read the letter carefully, and promptly tore it up. The astonished employee stared back at Watson and asked, "I've just lost 10 million dollars for this company aren't you going to fire me?"

"Absolutely not!" Watson replied, "I've just spent 10 million dollars on your education and you're much too valuable to this organization for me to let you go now."

Failure, mistake, fiasco, bomb, dud, flop, turkey, garbage, junk, reject, scrap, setback, breakdown, screw up, blunder, blooper, foul-up, bungle, faux pas.

These are just some of the words that we use when things just don't turn out the way we had planned or hoped or imagined. Look closely at those words. They are all value judgments. They describe an outcome of an action in a very negative way.

Whenever you do anything, you create a result. A failure is just a result that you hadn't anticipated. But we rarely look at this unanticipated result in a positive way. We certainly don't describe it as a learning experience. But when we look at failures as learning experiences, they can actually help us to become more successful.

Thomas Edison experimented with about 3,000 different ways to invent the light bulb until he finally came up with the filament material that worked for him. Was each one of those 2,999 initial combinations a failure? No, they just didn't produce the results Edison wanted.

Edison was interviewed later in his career, at a point when he had tried about 5,000 different ways to build an electric storage battery to store the electricity that powered his light bulbs. The reporter asked him, "Mr. Edison, you've been eminently successful for many, many years. You've made millions of dollars for yourself and for other people. How does it feel to be a failure so late in your career?"

> "It is a mistake to suppose that [people] succeed through success; they much oftener succeed through failure."
>
> SAMUEL SMILES

> "The way to succeed is to double your failure rate."
>
> THOMAS WATSON, JR.,

Edison turned to the reporter and smiled, "Young man you know very little about the world. For I have not failed, rather I know 5,000 ways not to invent a storage battery, and I'm that much closer to my goal." Edison was a master at using his "mistakes" as stepping stones to discovery.

The quality movement in this country has done remarkable things to strengthen the economic vitality of many companies and to convince disgruntled Americans to buy American products again. One of the axioms of the quality movement is, "Do it right the first time every time." Watch out! There is a problem if you run your business based solely on this principle.

D on't get me wrong. Doing things absolutely right is crucial. However, the problem comes when we use this quality principle too early. Unfortunately, the tendency is for people to apply the principle too soon. They start trying to "do it right the first time every time" when they are still generating ideas and attempting to solve problems. That's the wrong time to "do it right." In fact, that's the time—in the planning and testing stages—to make mistakes. Lots of them. Only by making lots of mistakes and learning from those unanticipated results will you be able to create the new products that can then be done right the first time, every time.

Burt Rutan is an airplane designer who, along with his wife Jeana Yeager, built the ultralight aircraft Voyager and flew it around the earth on one tank of gas. He has this to say about failure: "I've got to develop nine prototypes that go nowhere to make one that goes to production for big money. Only the place that tolerates failure gives rise to the thinking that results in success."

C reativity flourishes in an environment that says it's okay to make some mistakes sometimes, or it's okay to try some new things. Part of being creative is making mistakes.

One of the techniques we use to help people feel comfortable and allow themselves to experiment with new ways for solving tough problems is to give everyone a mistake quotient. They have at least 30 mistakes to make... and if they make 30 mistakes, they get them 30 more. It is amazing how the participation increases when people realize they wouldn't be ridiculed if their idea or their performance isn't just perfect.

 So don't be so hard on yourself. After all, some of the most creative and effective people of our time have made some major blunders. Give yourself some permission to make some mistakes, because if you're not making some mistakes, you're not making any discoveries. ✳

Doing things absolutely right is crucial. The problem comes when we use this "quality" principle too early.

Remember Tom Peters' three keys to business success: 1) test fast, 2) fail fast, 3) adjust fast.

The Myth of Radical Creativity

Is only the radical breakthrough creative?

We're here to shatter an American myth: that the only way to be "creative" is to come up with a breakthrough that no one ever dreamed of before, that conventional wisdom said was impossible, that radically changes the world as we know it. This sort of breakthrough might include the Wright flyer, Alexander Graham Bell's telephone and Edison's light bulb. Mind you, we have nothing against them.

But what would have happened if those new breakthroughs were never improved or refined? Think about it. Would you rather fly to Europe on a Wright Flyer or in a 747?

The answer is obvious. (If the answer is not obvious to you, please call the FAA.) But to most people a 747 doesn't seem as creative as the Wright brothers' airplane. Why not? Because it's not sexy, flashy or brand new. The Boeing 747 is an incremental improvement that has occurred over time.

The American view of creativity is: the big hit, the home run, the big bang, the instant profit. But creativity is not only the big breakthrough. Creativity is also improving, refining and crafting ideas. Home runs are important, but the game can also be won with a series of singles.

This home run view of creativity has been extremely detrimental to American business. The technology for the fax machine was invented in the United States but it wasn't taken to market because the cost of making it commercially viable seemed prohibitive. Today almost every American office has a fax machine. However, none are made in the United States. All are made in Japan or other Pacific Rim countries. Not commercially viable? It was the Japanese that took the long view and improved and refined facsimile technology to make it profitable.

Video technology was originally invented in the USA. However, it was also too expensive to develop and market in a short period of time. Today most American households have one or more VCR's, but there are very few, if any, made in the USA.

So what's the problem? Is it the impatience of Americans? Is it our short-term, quarterly-profit mentality? That's only part of the problem. Another reason is our view of creativity.

> Would you rather fly to Europe on a Wright Flyer or in a 747?

> The American view of creativity is the big hit, the home run, the big bang, the instant profit.

Creativity Resources

Michael Kirton, a researcher in the United Kingdom has developed a continuum that identifies two types of creativity: 1) adaptive creativity and 2) innovative creativity.

Adaptive creativity is working within the system to help things run smother, make them more cost-effective and more efficient. Adaptive creativity focuses on incrementally improving the quality of an already existing product or process.

Innovative creativity breaks the pattern of traditionally accepted behavior or beliefs. Innovative creativity challenges the status quo and breaks with the traditional world view to introduce new, often radical approaches.

Can you guess what type of creativity the Wright Flyer was? You got it, innovative. They proved that humans can fly, shattering the widely held assumption of the day. However, it was adaptive creativity that improved the airplane to make it more comfortable, safer and commercially viable. Likewise, innovative creativity came up with the facsimile and video technology, but it was adaptive creativity that brought this technology to market and made it profitable.

Kirton's theory actually originated by identifying individuals in organizations that naturally expressed innovative creativity or adaptive creativity. He found that some people were excellent at coming up with ideas to improve the current system, while others were good at creating ideas that challenged or changed the system. When these two types of people work together effectively to solve problems, the results can be astounding. However, as you might have guessed, adaptors and innovators see the world very differently. Without mutual respect and understanding, collaborating can often lead to war instead of effective problem solving. Kirton's personality assessment, the Kirton Adaption Innovation inventory, is a helpful tool for members of work teams to gain an understanding of the strengths each group brings to the table.

The bottom line is that both types of creativity are important. It is crucial for organizations to support innovative breakthroughs, and it is also important to nurture the patient, long-view, adaptive creativity that is necessary to make breakthroughs commercially viable. Since people naturally express their creativity in different ways, businesses can increase their success by supporting both innovative and adaptive creativity. ✳

What You Think is the Problem...

...is probably not the problem.

Albert Einstein was once asked, if some imminent disaster threatened the world, and he had one hour in which he knew he could save it, how would he spend his time.

Einstein thought for a minute and then replied, "I would spend the first 55 minutes identifying the problem and the last five minutes solving it. For the formulation of a problem is often far more essential that its solution, which may be merely a matter of mathematical or experimental skill."

Think about the last time you tackled a tough problem in your business or your personal life. How did you spend your time? Did you immediately race off to take action on what you thought was a solution to your problem, only to discover later that what you thought was the problem was not the problem after all, and the action that you took was ineffective?

One of the major misconceptions about creativity is that the only "place" to be creative is in the development of novel ideas for solving a problem. However, a great deal of creativity is necessary to help us discover the real problem. One way to be more effective in your business or personal life is to consciously work to understand your problem before you generate ideas or take action to solve it.

A classic story of solving the wrong problem occurred several years ago when a semi-tractor trailer truck got stuck as it tried to pass under a low clearance train trestle. The truck made it about half of the way under the train trestle before the top of the trailer wedged itself tightly into place. The truck could not more forward or backward. It was stuck.

Engineers and construction workers were brought in with cranes and other heavy equipment to dismantle part of the trestle, which would free the truck. A small crowd gathered to watch the activity. In the crowd was a boy about 11 years old. He watched the impressive undertaking. Suddenly he noticed something, and pushed himself through the crowd to the foreman who was directing the dismantling of the trestle.

"Hey mister, I think I know how to get the truck out of there."
"Yeah, sure kid," the foreman replied, "I don't have time to talk to you now. Can't you see I'm busy?"

> "...the formulation of a problem is often far more essential that its solution."
>
> ALBERT EINSTEIN

Creativity Resources

The young boy persisted. "But mister, I really do know how to get the truck out." Finally, in desperation, and to be left alone, the foreman turned to the youngster. "OK, smart guy. How would you do this job?"

The truck is too high to fit under the trestle, right?"
"Yes." the foreman replied gruffly.
"And you are trying to raise the trestle, right?"
"Yes."
"Well, why don't you try lowering the truck?"
"What do you mean?" the foreman asked.
"Why don't you let some of the air out of the tires? That will lower the truck and you can probably back it out."

Should we make the bridge higher? Or the truck lower?

Of course you know how this story ends. A sufficient amount of air was released from the truck tires, which lowered the truck enough so that it could be easily backed out from under the trestle.

The breakthrough in this problem didn't happen by generating more ideas to solve the problem as it was initially understood, but by redefining the problem from "How might we make the bridge higher?" to "How might we make the truck lower?"

So, how do you change your approach to problem "finding?" First the language you use when you describe a problem is crucial. Describe your problem in such a way that your mind considers it possible to solve, not as an obstacle. To help you view the problem as a challenge that can be solved, it is helpful to phrase it like a question. We recommend using phrases like: "How might we....," "How to....," "In what ways might we..." or "What might be all the...?"

Instead of describing your problem as "We don't have any money to develop this project," try phrasing the problem as "how might we reduce the cost of this project?" or "How might we raise the money?" The last two phrases describe a problem that can be solved. The first statement will block your thinking.

Next, just as it is crucial to generate many ideas for solving a problem, it is essential to generate many ways to approach the problem. Take out a legal pad and write your first impression of the problem beginning with a "How might we..." or an "In what ways might I..." Don't judge any of the challenge questions you think of and challenge yourself to write down at least 30 ways to restate the problem.

At first you will probably find this activity uncomfortable. This is because most of the previous training we have had in our lives has taught us that as soon as we thought we knew what the "problem" was, we immediately needed to come up with the one right answer to solve it. However, the purpose of generating many different challenge questions is not to solve the problem right away, but to develop a more effective definition of the problem.

One of the reasons you will probably find it uncomfortable to generate many different problem definitions is that as you were getting your education, from elementary school to college, you were taught that there was only one right answer to a problem: Two plus two always equals four. You were also taught that the quicker you got the right answer, the smarter you were.

"This Quick Solution Syndrome" continued as you went into business. The sign of a successful manager is one who is decisive and always has the right answer. You learned that as soon as you discovered a problem, you had to solve it, immediately. Problem. Solve it. You were not taught that valuable time was actually lost by not taking an active approach to discovering the true problem. When you spend time consciously challenging your first impression of the problem, you receive great dividends when you discover and then solve the real problem.

Try it. Next time you have a tough problem to solve, don't immediately rush right out to solve it. In fact, the tougher the problem, the more important it is to consciously focus to redefine it. Take out your legal pad. Number your page from one to 30. Phrase your problem beginning with the words "How to….., "How might I…..," "In what ways might I…" or "What might be all the…?"

Don't judge any of the challenge questions you generate until you have at least 30. Review the different approaches to your problem, and watch the real problem reveal itself to you. Remember: remove the truck, don't move the bridge. *

Don't judge any of the challenge questions you generate until you have at least 30.

The Value of Data

Fighting the urge to solve the problem before you know what it's about!

When most people think about solving problems creatively, they think about generating solutions. Yet preparing the mind to solve problems is an important first step. And in order to prepare the mind, it is important to understand the situation fully by learning everything you can.

The Five "W's"

Gathering data starts by opening your mind to actively seek out all the facts, feelings, questions, knowns and unknowns about a situation. The questions that will help you in the search are the old reporter's standbys: Who, What, Where, When, Why, and How. Lurking within this data you may find obvious, simple, and elegant solutions to the problem. Or you may even find some opportunities!

A Drug for the Heart?

For example, Viagara, the number one income producer for Pfizer Pharmaceuticals was developed by mistake. It was originally developed for and being tested as a heart drug. Unfortunately, as a heart drug, it didn't work, so the clinical trial was cancelled. Yet hidden in the data that pointed out the product's failure was an unplanned yet very marketable "side-effect." The message: Pay attention to the data, even if it's not telling you what you're expecting to hear.

Killing Two Diseases With One Stone

Prior to the 1940's most patients admitted to psychiatric hospitals for schizophrenia stayed there for the rest of their lives, since an unmedicated schizophrenia was not safe in the community. Drugs at the time rendered patients insensible and able to do only the most routine functions. Individuals on therapeutic doses of these drugs were therefore unable to manage community based living. There was no better alternative.

Enter the clinical trials for antihistamines, a class of drugs being developed in the thirties for the same purpose they're used today…combating allergies. As was a common practice at the time, late phase clinical trials were conducted on "captive" groups, such as military personnel, prisoners, and hospitalized psychiatric patients. As the antihistamines were administered to the psychiatric patients, there seemed to also be a decrease of "acting out" behaviors, if not a decrease of the psychosis itself. Researchers initially assumed it to be a Hawthorne effect (improvement of the patient due to increased interaction with an attentive caregiver/researcher). Yet the antipsychotic effect seemed to persist for a period of time beyond what one would expect.

The Best Thing Since Moldy Bread?

More data was gathered and researchers worked for over ten years to increase the antipsychotic effect of the drug. The first approved compound (chlorpromazine) was synthesized in 1950 and sold as Thorazine by Smith, Kline & French. Some scholars point to its introduction as a major breakthrough in the field of psychopharmacology, on par with the introduction of penicillin for major infectious diseases.

As if that's not enough, as researchers gathered more data and were open to "additional findings," an opportunity was found to help people in a previously unintended way, leading to tri-cyclic antidepressants. But it's not just limited to drug manufacturing. At a plant that makes material for counter-top surfaces, they faced a very strange challenge.

Gray Counter-tops Cause Gray Hair for Engineer

For no apparent reason, every now and then a batch of counter tops that were supposed to be white would turn out gray! Detailed analysis of the process and ingredients showed no differences in the batches that turned out white and those that turned out gray, so they turned loose an engineer to find out what the problem was. The engineer started talking to people, looking at where the supplies were stored, tracing the shipments or raw materials, looking at the equipment, and so on. But he kept running into dead ends until he explored the facility, inside... and out. While walking around the roof, he noticed to the northeast of the production facility there was an automotive manufacturing plant.

Normally this wasn't a problem, because at the facility, the wind almost always blows from the west, off of the lake. Yet when he did an analysis of the days when the bad batches of counter tops were produced and compared them to the weather data, he discovered an exact correlation of bad batches to winds from the northeast. As it turns out, the soot from the automotive plant smokestacks next door was contaminating the batches through the air intakes and changing the color. This led to the successful implementation of a solution that solved the problem.

Understand Everything (even dumb literary references)

So remember: before rushing into generate ideas, make sure you fully understand the problem. You may want to picture the engineer on the rooftop trying to solve the mystery of the gray counter tops. You might even call this story, A Portrait of Corian® Gray!

How to Keep your Creativity Fresh

Creative thinking and Creative Problem Solving tools help spawn a proliferation of ideas and fresh thinking. But after a while, it's not uncommon for people to find that their "flowing river of ideas" has been reduced to a trickle. So how can we keep our creativity renewed and revitalized on a daily basis? Try out the eight specific suggestions listed below:

Use active ways to generate ideas.

There are explicit, tested approaches for generating ideas. One of the best active methods is Brainstorming, the group creative problem solving technique developed by advertising executive Alex Osborn, which he shared in his book *Applied Imagination*. To use brainstorming effectively, follow the four guidelines on which it is based. Those guidelines are:

1) Defer judgment. Don't evaluate your ideas while you are generating them. Whatever ideas come to mind, write them down — all of them! They will be evaluated later.

2) Strive for quantity. The more ideas you come up with, the greater are your chances of getting a good one. One of the best ways to apply this guideline is to establish an idea quota. I've found it helpful to set a goal of about 35 to 40 ideas. This quota seems to be high enough to purge out the usual approaches to solving the problem but still stretches you into new concept areas. Don't stop at the quota if you are really generating good ideas. If your problem is fairly complicated, establish a higher quota of ideas. Let yourself go and you will be very pleased with the ideas you develop after you reach your goal. And if you haven't solved your problem when you reach your quota, double the target and keep going.

3) Seek wild and unusual ideas—the wilder the better. Alex Osborn said that it is easier to tame down a wild idea than to invigorate a weak one. The implication is that we need to strive to create some wild, unusual ideas, since they can always be engineered down later.

4) Build on other ideas. Let one idea spur other ideas. One of the most common approaches to creativity is to make incremental improvements to already existing ideas by building on them. Small improvements are important because they lead to better, more refined ideas. In a brainstorming session, the ideas you generate are just starting points. Allow yourself and others to build on and improve those ideas.

Do you always need a group to brainstorm? Absolutely not. The four brainstorming rules can also be applied individually.

Use passive ways to generate ideas.

Most of us don't get our best ideas at work. People usually report that they get their best ideas while driving a car, taking a bath or shower or as they are falling asleep at night.

While at work, most of us are in the implementation mode, the action mode, the make-it-happen mode. New ideas begin to surface when we get away from work and are able to pay attention to something in an almost automatic, relaxed way. It seems that activities like driving, bathing or falling asleep are so automatic that we relax the judgmental part of our thinking, which in turn allows new ideas to surface.

The key is to be ready to catch those ideas when they appear. Have a piece of paper, a note pad or a pocket tape recorder with you to record those new insights as soon as they occur. If you don't write it down right away, it might just disappear.

A friend of mine calls his answering machine with his new ideas so he can listen to them when he gets back to his office. Use whatever method works for you to capture your fortuitous insights.

Look for the strengths in a new concept first.

When you are presented with an idea, or after you have generated a number of ideas, the next step is to evaluate and/or refine them. Unfortunately, most of us "refine" an idea by first examining all the things that are wrong it. One of the techniques I use in my creativity seminars is to encourage participants to evaluate ideas by looking at the pluses, potentials and concerns of an idea, then overcoming their concerns. I call it Praise First or POINt for short. Here's how it works:

1) After you've selected an idea you'd like to develop and implement, list at least three things that are good about the idea. Those are the Pluses.

2) Then list the opportunities: speculations or possible future gains that might result if the idea were implemented. Try starting these with "It might...."

3) No idea is perfect so, as your third step, list the issues you have about your idea. But phrase those issue as questions, or challenge questions so that you continue the idea development process by inviting solutions. If your issue is that the idea will cost too much, rephrase this concern as "How to reduce the cost?" or "How to find the money to develop the idea?"

4) With your issue about the idea phrased as questions, you can now generate new thinking to overcome the issues, strengthen your idea and increase its chances for acceptance. This is a positive pro-active approach to evaluating and building ideas.

George Leonard in his book *Mastery* stressed the importance of acknowledging the negative, but accentuating the positive. Telling people what they are doing wrong while ignoring what they're doing right reduces their energy. The same is true for ideas, and that's why Praise First (POINt) works.

Vary your routine.

It's no surprise that many of us get great ideas for work related problems when we are on vacation. When you go on vacation, your routine is significantly altered. You aren't keeping your regular hours. You aren't in the familiar surroundings. You aren't exposed to the situations that face you at a usual work day. One of my colleagues, Gerard Puccio says that there is a direct relationship between the distance he is away from home and the number of new ideas he generates. For Gerard, the farther away from home, the more new ideas he generates.

Now, I'm not suggesting that every time you need to come up with a new concept you leave town, but there are some definite ways to adapt this approach. Here are a couple of them:

Treat your commute time as a scenic vacation. Instead of thinking about what is going to happen at the office, focus on the world around you and take a mini-vacation on the way to work. Drive to work a different way, or get off the expressway and take the scenic route. By exposing yourself to some different scenery you are likely to get some new input. Ride the train to work? Then sit on the side opposite where you usually sit and look out the window instead of burying your nose in your book, files, or morning paper.

Vary your routine at work. Rather than do the same thing for lunch at the same place with the same people, go somewhere new with people you don't normally speak with. Bring in new pictures for your work area, or exchange them with the ones from your home every few months. Rearrange your office every quarter to get a new perspective. You'll also send a message to your co-workers that you're not trapped in a rut and are open to new ways of looking at things.

Vary your routine at home. Do you always go to the same place on Friday night for dinner? Do you always go to a movie on the weekend? Try a different approach. Don't go to a movie, go to a hockey game. Or stay home. Or take a walk. Have a barbecue on a boat. Never seen a foreign film? Go see a movie with subtitles.

John Gardner in his book *On Leadership*, discussed some of the ways that leaders handle stress. One of the ways is to change their routine. The leaders he interviewed had some favorite environment or pastime— a beach for walks, a stream for fishing. However, Gardner was struck by the fact that most of their solutions could be summed up in a brief line of advice: "Do something nonverbal." Music, nature, sensory enjoyment, working with one's hands, gardening or sports.

Read and listen to different material.

Several years ago Donna Hamlin of Hamlin, Harkin, Ltd. in San Jose, California, conducted a study on the reading habits of scientists. She grouped the scientists into three categories: The first group of scientists she labeled "innovative." These scientists were the ones who exhibited the highest creative productivity as measured by patents. The second group she labeled "productive" scientists. These scientists were known for being highly technically proficient scientists. The third group were scientists who were neither productive or innovative. The term used to identify this group was..."slugs."

The results of the study found that the "slugs" hardly read anything at all. The "productive" scientists read almost exclusively in their field. The highly creative scientists, however, while not always as technically updated as their counterparts in the second group, read in a variety of fields. In fact, a great deal of their reading was outside of their areas of expertise. These scientists were reading everything from science fiction to technical journals; from *Popular Mechanics* to the *National Inquirer*.

As you might imagine, the "innovative" group of scientists had a much richer storehouse of information from which to generate new concepts.

Don't have time to read? Listen to tapes in your car. But don't just listen to tapes that focus on your particular business. Buy self improvement tapes, books on tape and mysteries. Most public libraries have a variety of cassettes you can borrow. The old radio dramas were wonderful for exciting listeners' imaginations. Use the rich resource of taped material available today whenever you are driving your car.

Always listen to the same radio station with the same music programming? Try an all news format station or something that features a tremendous range of subjects such as *National Public Radio*. Use your drive time to keep your mind fresh and refreshed. And of course, keep that note book or tape recorder nearby so when those ideas surface, you can effortlessly record them.

Network.

In addition to reading and listening to different material, it's important to interact with different people. Most of us find it more comfortable to spend time with the people that are familiar to us. We don't make the time or effort to meet new people.

Research conducted on communication networks tells us that the best source of new information is not from the people you see on a regular basis — they usually have the same information you do. The best source of new information is from other networks— other, different people. This is also known as "non-homogeneous groups." To keep your creativity fresh, it is important to tap into groups of people that you usually don't interact with. Find those new networks and plug into them.

Stop the Action.

In our culture, the peace of solitude is difficult to attain. We are constantly bombarded with things to do, to buy and to take action on. However, all great leaders and teachers have taken time out of their busy schedule for meditation, rest and reflection.

The enlightenment that came to the Buddha while he was meditating under a tree on the banks of the Nairanjana river is said to have been the culmination of long reflection upon the human condition. Jesus spent forty days in the wilderness undergoing temptation by the devil before returning to proclaim his message of salvation. It is said that Ghandi spent from midnight on Sunday night to midnight Monday night in solitude, fasting, prayer and meditation.

When you remove yourself from your habitual, fast paced environment of day-to-day life, new self understanding is possible. Anthony Storr in his book *Solitude: A return to the self-reported Admiral Byrd's account of manning an Antarctic advanced weather base in the winter of 1934 as a form of renewal.* Byrd said, "I wanted something more than just privacy in the geographical sense. I wanted to sink roots into some replenishing philosophy. [I wanted] to be by myself for a while and to taste peace and quiet and solitude long enough to find out how good they really are." Byrd summed up the experience of his long solitude in Antarctica as, "I did take away something that I had not fully possessed before; an appreciation of the sheer beauty and miracle of being alive, and a humble set of values... I live more simply now, and with more peace."

Any form of solitude will work. Spend 30 minutes sitting quietly in a comfortable chair. Don't read, listen to music, eat or watch television. Just sit. In the first 10 minutes your mind will still be racing and will tell you all the things you should be doing. Resist the temptation to get up and act. This is your renewal time. After those first excruciating ten minutes, sitting in solitude will become easier. New insights might come forth. However, the important thing is to take a "time out" in your life. If you want some new ideas, you need to make some space for them. By stopping the action, you create room for those new ideas to come in.

One of the methods I use to take time out is to sit quietly on my porch and just gaze out over my tree-lined backyard. Don't have the opportunity to sit quietly at home for more than 30 seconds? Then try the approach that my friend uses. He will often leave work early and stop at a park near his home. He will sit in his car, gazing quietly out over the park for 30 minutes. He reports that this method works extraordinarily well for him. He gets some time to renew himself, to reflect and he doesn't create an imposition on his family or business associates.

Change your attitude about failure.

Whenever you do anything, you create a result. A failure is just a result that you didn't anticipate. Unfortunately, we rarely look at this unanticipated result in a positive way. However, if we look at failures as learning experiences, they can actually help us to become more creative.

Joe Louis said, "Everyone's got to figure to get beat sometime. "As John Gardner in his book *On Leadership* emphasized, "The question is not 'Did you take a fall?' but 'Did you get up and continue?'" Successful, creative people take criticism and failure, and use it to grow. They know that the book of life has many chapters.

As James Michener, the prolific, prize winning author once said, "I like challenge. I don't mind defeat. I don't gloat over victories. I want to stay in the ball game." ✳

CPS Success Stories from the Real World:
Inventing Profit at Kraft

Aggressive profit goals made it necessary to get creative about reducing expenses. Her assignment was to run a brainstorming session for 300 people that would deliver millions of dollars in savings.

Walking into the office of Debra Giampoli, director of consumer promotions with the New Meals Division at Kraft Foods in Glenview, Illinois, there's no question about where she stands on the issue of creativity. Toys and multi-colored gadgets line her bookshelves. Hand drawn pictures hang on the wall. But this has not always been the case. "I used to think work was not a place to be creative, that creativity was only for the weekends," she admits. What accounted for the change in attitude?

One contributing factor was the four days she spent learning to facilitate the Creative Problem Solving process. Since then, she has found herself in high demand for her facilitation services at Kraft. "I think they are coming to me because there is a tremendous need for creative process, and there are not many people who know how to do it comfortably," she says. Working mainly on marketing and promotional projects, Deb was successfully guiding small groups through the creative process.

Getting creative about reducing expenses
Then, one August, things took on a larger scale. The vice president of marketing and consumer promotions, knowing her reputation, called her into his office. Aggressive profit goals made it necessary for the division to get creative about ways to reduce expenses. He had arranged an off-site meeting in two weeks. Her assignment was to structure a division-wide brainstorming session for 300 people that would deliver millions of dollars in savings during the remaining months of that year and into the next.

Leverage everyone's best thinking
Rather than leave the cost cutting to the high-level officers, the leaders of the New Meals Division took a vastly different approach. "We wanted to rally all the troops," Deb says, "One of our division values is leveraging the value of teams and individuals. We really wanted to hold a division-wide session to address this genuine business need."

Deb had two weeks to pull it off. With the help of her original CPS facilitation trainer, she designed a three-hour crash course in Creative Problem Solving for 29 hand-picked facilitators. "I didn't want to diminish Creative Problem Solving to something that could be done on the back of a match book," says Deb, "but I thought, even if I can teach them just one tool, it will make them more productive." The crash course went off without a hitch. The 29 facilitators—chosen on the basis of leadership ability, energy level and creative sense—got a brief introduction to Creative Problem Solving and a few techniques to guide small group in cost savings ideas.

Business as fun

Deb and her team's ultimate creative coup was the theme for the event. This corporate meeting would not be a meeting at all, but rather, "The Battle of the Bands." On the morning of the event, Deb and her team made a deliberate effort to establish a playful atmosphere that would be energetic, engaging and productive. Each facilitator became the leader of a band such as the Doobie Brothers, INXS, the Rat Pack or the Rolling Stones. "We gave them musically themed graphics to hang on the walls in their rooms. They all had their own boom box and CD's, and music played freely," she says.

Cash prizes

There were 29 rooms, one team per room, and Deb floated in and out, encouraging participation and acknowledging the participants for their efforts. Deb and the team she worked with also put together a significant prize pool worth thousands of dollars. Awards included the Best Album for 1998, which went to the team with the highest 1998 saving idea, and the Lifetime Achievement Award for the team with the highest saving idea that would be ongoing year after year. Every participant got a gift certificate for a free CD.

Ideas: screened, banked, scheduled

What came of the thousands of ideas they generated? The ideas went through a feasibility screen manned by director-level managers whose job was "to reality check them," says Deb, "because we didn't want to be awarding prizes to people for ideas that we would never be able to apply." Even after a critical screening, the ideas totaled up to millions of dollars in potential savings. "The whole day was considered a huge success," she says.

It's more than just brainstorming

Deb credits the Creative Problem Solving Process, saying, "It got us to a place where we could identify some potential that had pretty big numbers associated with it. We like this process better than some of the more tactical brainstorming approaches because it starts sooner and ends later. So it is more than just techniques for brainstorming, it's techniques for solving problems." ✳

> "We like this process better than some of the more tactical brainstorming approaches because it starts sooner and ends later. So it is more than just techniques for brainstorming, it's techniques for solving problems."
>
> DEBRA GIAMPOLI

Creativity Resources

CPS Success Stories from the Real World:
Package Design at Clorox

Creative Problem Solving (CPS) is an effective process with many applications. The research and anecdotal evidence that testifies to its success is vast. One area where it has been used successfully in business is the area of designing packaging in which to ship consumer products. Just ask Jeff Harris, a Senior Engineer in the packaging dynamics laboratory of The Clorox Company.

Bottom-line results

According to Jeff, when designing packaging for a product, it is essential to look for cost savings since packaging adds costs to products. So, it makes sense that if you can reduce the amount of money spent for packing a product, you can essentially increase profits, or lower the price to help sell more product and increase market share.

By using the principles of CPS, Jeff was able to reduce what it cost to package a product from $7.64 to $3.27. Which is especially good, since the packaging design that cost $7.64 failed to protect the contents from damage.

How to achieve a 50% reduction in your costs

So how did Jeff improve the quality and reliability of the packaging through his application of creative problem solving? It all started when Jeff was transferred from his job as an analytical chemist, which he held for 15 years, to the protective packaging area. At that time, Clorox sent him to a training program on packaging design:

"It was an outside training class, a generic program and I was sent to be introduced to the process of packaging design. Our objective in the class was to design a protective package for a specialty computer which had a part that was subject to breakage in the distribution environment (i.e. when it was shipped UPS or Federal Express)."

"Over-packaging in this case was responsible for the product failures in the field. Excessive packing amplified the vibrations that occurred while the computer was riding in the back of an 18 wheel tractor-trailer rig across the country. The vibrations damaged the computer."

"We were divided into teams to work on this problem. Some of the teams jumped immediately to trying to find the cause, and they didn't spend any time trying to agree on a challenge question."

Putting on your armor

"I think some of the training that I've received in creativity and innovation helped protect me in the sense that the other participants in the workshop used 'killer phrases' when ideas were generated. I 'put my armor' on and looked at things from a different perspective. I tried to find more than one right answer."

"Some of the folks in the course didn't look for more than one right answer. When they found a 'right answer,' they stopped. But I continued to look at options that might be more radical and tried to change the paradigm a bit. Of course, the more radical the approach, the more likely one will have a breakthrough, and, in this case it would be a huge cost savings.

That won't work, or will it?

"In the workshop, we had to work with a material that had never been used in packaging design. People looked at it and said, 'Well, the static stress is 10 times too high.' Also, this material was delivered in a certain format: either a 4-inch block or a 4-inch sheet. When other participants looked at the material they would say, 'Well, Jeez, the weight of the computer doesn't justify its use; it's out of line.' And they would discard it But I would say, 'No, what that means to me is that I can use only one-tenth of the amount and achieve the same thing. The static stress will then be in line with what I need to protect the computer." When Jeff proposed using this material in his particular design, his ideas did not win immediate acceptance.

Convincing the skeptics

"Some people don't act like team members. They fold their arms and send the signal that they are not going to put any energy into the idea because they 'know' the idea won't work. There was one fellow in this group from a very innovative company who spent more time discrediting other people than congratulating them. So, I decided I wasn't going to be meek and modest. I'm going to be a warrior if I have to . That's what putting on the 'suit of armor' is all about. It's about not letting people get to you, even if they are throwing lots of killer phrases."

"Anyway we tested the idea in spite of the fact that there were still some folks who said it wouldn't work, and didn't want to go along with it. But once the initial tests showed it was possible, everyone got on board."

Success Secrets

When Jeff was asked what made this breakthrough successful, he mentioned four things which sum up the secret of his success at Clorox: He took the time to re-define the problem. He didn't accept the problem as it was initially proposed to him. He looked for more than one right answer to solve the problem, instead of stopping when he came up with just one solution. He intentionally tried to challenge the traditionally accepted paradigm of packaging with a different material. When the killer phrases came his way, he "put on his armor" and didn't let those phrases get him —or his ideas —down. ✳

> "Some of the folks in the course didn't look for more than one right answer. When they found a 'right answer,' they stopped."
>
> JEFF HARRIS

CPS Success Stories from the Real World:
Teaming at Sherrit

Robb LaBranche and Greg McGlone have set an ambitious target of saving $5 million in five years in the department in which Greg works. The two are committed employees of Sherrit Inc., a diversified public company based in Alberta, Canada, with 1700 employees and $1.5 billion in assets. They are doing some great work in implementing a work redesign which three years into the project is achieving tremendous success — both financially and from a quality of life perspective — for the department and its employees.

The initiative

Robb, the organizational development specialist, launched the initiative by identifying team-based problem-solving as a crucial component of the department's goal of moving from working in functional groups to cross-functional teams where maintenance, operations, and engineering support personnel worked together everyday.

Shortly after the department work redesign was implemented, Robb and the department's management team delivered department-wide training in the basics of problem-solving. Two years later, volunteer employees were trained as Creative Problem Solving (CPS) facilitators and then the entire department (about 100 people) received two days of CPS basic training.

Blair Miller conducted the CPS training and worked with Jonathan Vehar to train the facilitators. Based on the success of the CPS training in the department, Robb rolled it out to the rest of the company by bringing in Roger Firestien to energize the company with his creativity program and sponsored additional introductory CPS and facilitation training. There is also a CPS facilitator network to support new facilitators.

Real-life problems

A critical part of the CPS basic training program was the inclusion of organizational problems to be solved during the training so that the participants could see first-hand how effectively CPS worked to solve problems they had been previously unable to solve. Some of the problems successfully addressed by the organization include:

- The need for a more flexible work and vacation schedule
- The opportunity to expand involvement in decision making
- Exploring ways to balance recognition and responsibility in people's jobs
- The need for a set of hiring criteria that would allow the organization to hire the best people for the department and the business

The participants also used CPS to work on issues regarding the annual plant shut-down and to plan and implement additional training programs.

Return on training investment

What about bottom line results? Shortly after initiating the training, the department ran into a major operational problem with one of the new lines that produced fertilizer. It was expected to produce 35 tons per hour, yet after 2 weeks, they couldn't get it to produce more than 28 tons per hour.

Three of the trained CPS facilitators took on the challenge at a Monday morning meeting. The three facilitators and 15 resource group members worked on the problem for two hours using CPS, then dedicated a five person team to work on the problem until 4:00 PM on Wednesday.

Within two days, the facility was up to the target of 35 tons per hour and after implementing all of the solutions that the team created, the facility is now producing 40 tons per hour. Since the product sells for $300 per ton, it's easy to see how this solution paid for the training program in a relatively short time.

Lessons learned from CPS training

Robb and Greg have worked on developing a creative, participative work environment for several years now. Here are a few tips for those considering a similar initiative:

• It's easy to deliver the training. The real challenge is having people take the next step to apply it to the workplace. More energy is required to apply the learnings than is required to deliver the training. But all of the benefits are in the application of the learnings.

• The organizational culture needs to give people the authority to solve problems, to be accountable, to work as a team. If the boss solves all of the problems, the subordinates have no energy to solve them.

• Conduct CPS training early. Incorporate it into the team development, since it is the key to solving problems and solving problems is the reasons the teams exist.

Keep up the good work

We will keep an eye on Robb and Greg as they continue their initiative. Clearly they are on the right track in developing creative, participative work environments that deliver bottom line results. We wish them continued success! ✳

"Create an environment where people will speak their thoughts and others will build upon them to solve problems and create new opportunities."

GREG MCGLONE

"Set time aside to be deliberately creative — take time to use the [CPS] process to be deliberately more creative."

ROBB LABRANCHE

"Create an environment that values diversity in thinking. Using the CPS process can help."

ROBB LABRANCHE

Creativity Resources

CPS Success Stories from the Real World:
Exploding Limitations at Mead

Would you like to be the first on your block to create a world-class product that will increase your customer mix, generate increased profits and save over half a million dollars per year? Dave Newcomer and the Mead Fine Paper's Papeterie Marketing group managed to accomplish this recently and redefine the standard for integrated mill paper products, or in Dave's words, produce a "Chevrolet type product with the quality of a Mercedes."

Developing an idea-friendly organization

The road to this breakthrough began when Roger started working with the group to teach them the tools and techniques necessary to work together creatively. The Marketing team began holding meetings every other Friday that led to a number of personnel breakthroughs and opportunities to practice the Praise First technique. The group learned Praise First through Roger's workshop and video and has integrated the process of looking at an idea's pluses and potentials without the idea slaughtering that is typical of group meetings.

The mission. Impossible?

Cut to a recent challenge offered up by one of their customers to produce a whiter, brighter paper. Paper brightness is measured by the percentage of light that it reflects. For example, a 100 bright paper reflects 100 percent of light shone on it, and is extremely difficult to accomplish. Until the challenge, Mead produced a paper with a 94 grade, and their competitor produced a 95. Dave's group decided to go for a 96 grade and establish a new standard.

The approach to making the old 94 grade paper was to "force" the existing production system which resulted in a paper with a pink shade that Mead was not very proud of. Dave says that to improve upon this, they created a, "Brightness Enhancement team made up of a very diverse cross-functional group. We have people on this team with educational backgrounds from high school to Doctorate degrees, people from machine crews to Mead Central Research. For this project, and for the first time in my experience here, we also used the expertise of one of our leading dye suppliers."

Hmm, training in creativity tools and techniques, plus a team of diverse perspectives that created a breakthrough. What else could you need?

Setting unattainable goals

Well, a few other elements were crucial. Dave noted that they spent some time developing a process that resulted in new application techniques that were new to the industry, radically different and yet much simpler and cost effective. Dave notes that he is "glad we set our sights higher than we thought we could go."

Yet it also required perseverance. The company spent most of a day producing paper that was not up to their specifications. They tweaked, argued, jury-rigged and convinced each other not to give up before they finally produced one roll of paper with a 99 brightness before the run settled down to a consistent 98 grade. To Dave's knowledge they produced, "the brightest sheet ever produced by an integrated mill like this. [It] was truly a momentous occasion."

Making the grade

He's justifiably excited: "Our grades went up four brightness points...We now have a world-class product. We created a win/win all the way around. This higher brightness product was cheaper to produce and was of greater value to our customer. Not only are our customers in the United States excited about this product, but our partners in the U.K., Austria and Germany are enamored with it as well."

Recipe for success

So here's the necessary ingredients for Mead's breakthrough:

1)   Proficiency with tools and techniques that aid creativity
2)   A group of people with diverse perspectives
3)   The desire to achieve standards higher than you think possible
4)   Hard work and perseverance
5)   The courage to make mistakes

Congratulations to Mead Fine Paper for having several bright ideas that resulted in a truly bright product. ✳

CPS Timeline

What your history teacher would tell you about CPS

Adam & Eve/Big Bang-1950:
Creativity is regarded as mysterious, magical, madness or from "the muses."

1950:
J.P. Guilford, president of the American Psychological Association, challenges his colleagues to study creativity.

1953:
Alex Osborn, founding partner of advertising agency BBDO (one of the largest in the world today) writes Applied Imagination, introducing the world to Brainstorming and a seven-step process called Creative Problem Solving. (His seven steps: Orientation, Preparation, Analysis, Hypothesis, Incubation, Synthesis and Verification)

1954:
Osborn founds the Creative Education Foundation.

1967:
The second edition of Applied Imagination (published posthumously) features a revised version of Creative Problem Solving: Fact-finding, Idea-finding and Solution-finding. Sidney Parnes released a further revised version of Creative Problem Solving resulting from his extensive work with Osborn and several other creativity professionals: Fact-finding, Problem-finding, Idea-finding, Solution-finding and Acceptance-finding.

1978:
Ruth Noller provides this definition: "**Creative**—having an element of newness and being relevant at least to you, the one who creates the solution; **Problem**—any situation which presents a challenge, offers an opportunity or is a concern to you; **Solving**—devising ways to answer or meet or satisfy the problem; adapting yourself to the situation or adapting the situation to yourself. **Creative Problem Solving**—a process, a method, a system for approaching a problem in an imaginative way resulting in effective action."

1981:
Bill Shephard and Roger Firestien identify the value of specific roles in problem solving sessions:
1) Facilitator: responsible for running the process
2) Client: responsible for owning the problem, making decisions and implementing the outcomes of the session
3) Resource Group: trained to provide creative input for the client

1982:
Diane Foucar-Szocki, Don Treffinger, Scott Isaksen and Roger Firestien develop a range of convergent tools to balance the prior focus on divergent tools and techniques.

1985:
Objective-finding is added as a sixth deliberate step, rather than an intuitive entry point by Parnes (A Facilitative Style of Leadership) and by Scott Isaksen and Don Treffinger (Creative Problem Solving: The Basic Course). Isaksen and Treffinger also develop explicit rules for convergent thinking.

1989:
Scott Isaksen and Don Treffinger break up the six stages into three components (similar to Osborn's 1967 three-step model) to reflect how people actually use the process: Understanding the Problem (made up of Mess-finding, Data-finding and Problem-finding), Generating Ideas (Idea-finding), Planning for Action (Solution-finding and Acceptance-finding).

1994-1995:
Blair Miller, Jonathan Vehar and Roger Firestien modify the process to make it easier to understand and to use in plain English

2001:
FourSight publishes "FourSight: The Breakthrough Thinking Profile," based on the work of Gerard Puccio, PhD, which uncovers the link between CPS and individual thinking preferences.

2010:
Dorte Nielsen and Sarah Thurber develop a visual model for FourSight which makes CPS even easier to teach and remember.

Now - The End of Time:
Continuous improvement makes the process easier to learn and use.

To Learn More...

Books

Eckert, R. and Vehar, J.R. (2007). *More Lightning, Less Thunder: How to Energize Innovation Teams. (3rd ed.)* Paul Smiths, NY: New & Improved.

Firestien, R.L. (1998). *Why Didn't I Think of That? A personal and professional guide to better ideas and decision making.* Williamsville, NY: Innovation Resources, Inc.

Firestien, R.L. (1996). *Leading on the Creative Edge: Gaining competitive advantage through the power of Creative Problem Solving.* Colorado Springs, CO: Piñon Press.

FourSight. (2006). *Your Thinking Profile.* Evanston, IL: FourSight.

FourSight. (2006). *Your Tool Cards.* Evanston, IL: FourSight.

FourSight. (2010). *Your Innovation Station.* Evanston, IL: FourSight.

Grivas, C. and Puccio, G.J. (2011). *The Innovative Team: Unleashing creative potential for breakthrough results.* San Francisco: Jossey-Bass.

May, R. (1976). *The Courage to Create.* New York, NY: Bantam Books.

Miller, B.J., Vehar, J.R. & Firestien, R.L., Thurber, S.B. and Nielsen, D.S. (2011). *Facilitation: A door to creative leadership.* Evanston, IL: FourSight.

Nielsen, D.S. (2011). *Inspired: How creative people think, work and find inspiration.* Amsterdam: BIS publishers.

Osborn, A.F. (1993). *Applied Imagination.* Buffalo, NY: Creative Education Foundation.

Parnes, S.J. (1997). *Optimize the Magic of Your Mind.* Buffalo, NY: Creative Education Foundation in association with Bearly Limited.

Parnes, S.J. (1988). *Visionizing.* Buffalo, NY: Creative Education Foundation.

Puccio, G.J. (2004). *FourSight: Your Thinking Profile,* Evanston, IL: FourSight.

Puccio, G.J., Mance, M. and Murdock, M.C. (2011) *Creative Leadership: Skills that drive change. (2nd ed.).* Thousand Oaks, CA: Sage.

Puccio, G.J. & Murdock, M.C. (Eds.) (1999). *Creativity Assessments. Readings and resources.* Buffalo, NY: Creative Education Foundation.

Ray, M. and Myers, R. (1986). *Creativity in Business.* Garden City, NY: Doubleday.

Shekerjian, D. (1990). *Uncommon Genius.* New York, NY: Viking Penguin.

VanGundy, A.B. (1992). *Idea Power: Techniques and Resources to Unleash the Creativity in Your Organization.* New York, NY: AMACOM.

Videos

Firestien, R.L., Vehar, J.R. and Chamberlain, S. (1998). *Applying Creativity Video Series* (10 videos). *Online at www.buffalostate.edu/creativity/x1184.xml*

Websites & Blogs

www.blairmiller.com
www.buffalostate.edu/centers/creativity
www.createresults.com
www.foursightonline.com
www.newandimproved.com
www.rogerfirestien.com

Sources

FourSight: Your Thinking Profile is available on the web at www.foursightonline.com.

More Lightning, Less Thunder is available at Amazon.com.

References Cited

Amabile, Teresa, et. al. (1995) KEYS: User's Guide. Greensboro, NC.: Center for Creative Leadership.

Amabile. T.M. (1983) The social psychology of creativity. New York: Springer-Verlag.

Battelle-Institut. (1972) Methoden und organization der ideenfindung in der industrie (Methods and organization of idea finding in industry). Frankfurt, Germany: Battelle.

Besemer, S.P. & Treffinger, D.J. (1981). Analysis of creative products: review and synthesis. Journal of Creative Behavior, 15, 158-178.

Black, R.A. (1998) Broken Crayons. Athens, GA. Cre8ng Places Press.

Brown, W.E. (May, 1972). "Praise-Criticism Ratio: Do teachers take advantage of it?" Behaviorally Speaking, 11.

Creative Thinking and Creative Problem Solving. (1994). Buffalo, NY: Creative Education Foundation.

Eberle, R. F. (1971) Scamper: Games for imagination development. Buffalo, NY:DOK.

Ekvall, G. (1996). Organizational Climate for Creativity and Innovation. European Journal of Work and Organizational Psychology, 5(1), 105-123.

Ekvall, G. (1983). Climate, structure and innovativeness of organizations: A theoretical framework and an experiment. Stockholm, Sweden: The Swedish Council for Management and Organizational Behaviour.

Firestien, R.L and Vehar, J.R. (1997). Insights into innovation. Buffalo, NY: Roger L. Firestien, Ph.D.

Firestien, R.L. (1996). Leading on the creative edge. Colorado Springs, CO: Pinon Press.

Firestien, R.L. (1988). From basics to breakthroughs: A guide to better thinking and decision-making. Williamsville, NY: Innovation Resources, Inc.

Firestien, R. L. (1983). Ownership and converging: Essential ingredients of Creative Problem Solving. Journal of Creative Behavior, 17(1), 32-38.

Gardner, J.W. (1990). On leadership. New York: Free Press.

Geschka, H. (1979). Methods and organization of idea generation. Creativity Week Two, 1979 Proceedings. Greensboro, N.C: Center for Creative Leadership.

Gordon, W. (1961). Synectics. New York: Harper & Row.

Gryskiewicz, S.S. (1980). Targeted innovation: a situational approach. In S.S. Gryskiewicz (ed.), Creativity Week 3, 1980 proceedings, (pp. 77-103). Greensboro, NC: Center for Creative Leadership.

Hayakawa, S.I. (1978). Language in thought and action, 4th edition. New York: Harcourt Brace Jovanovich.
Isaksen, S. G., Dorval, K. B., & Treffinger, D. J. (1994). Creative approaches to problem solving. Dubuque, IA.: Kendall/Hunt Publishing Company.

Isaksen, S.G. & Treffinger, D.J. (1985). Creative Problem Solving: The basic course. Buffalo, NY: Bearly Limited.

Korzybski, A. (1933). Science and sanity, an introduction to non-Aristotelin systems and general semantics. (publisher unknown).

McLean, P.D. (1973). A triune concept of the brain and behavior. Toronto, Ontario: University of Toronto Press.

Meier, D. (2000). The accelerated learning handbook. New York, NY: McGraw-Hill.

Michalko, M. (1991). Thinkertoys. Berkeley, CA: Ten Speed.

Miller, B.J., Avarello, L.L., Coleman, S.E., Puccio, G.J., & Vehar, J.R. (1994). CPS in action. Chicago: Blair J. Miller.

Osborn, A. F. (1953). Applied imagination: Principles and procedures of Creative Problem Solving. New York: Scribner's.

Osborn, A. F. (1993). Applied imagination: Principles and procedures of Creative Problem Solving (3rd ed.). Buffalo, NY: The Creative Education Foundation Press.

Parnes, S.J. (1988). Visionizing. Buffalo, NY: Creative Education Foundation.

Parnes, S.J. (1985). A facilitating style of leadership. Buffalo, NY: Bearly Limited.

Parnes, S.J. (1981). The magic of your mind. Buffalo, NY: The Creative Education Foundation.

Parnes, S.J. (1967). Creative behavior guidebook. New York: Charles Scribner's Sons.

Rhodes, M. (1961). "An analysis of creativity." Phi Delta Kappan, 42, 305-310.

Treffinger, D.J. & Firestien, R.L. (1983). "Ownership and converging: Essential ingredients of Creative Problem Solving." Journal of Creative Behavior, 17(1), 32-38.

Treffinger,D.J., Isaksen, S.G., Firestien, R.L.(1982). Handbook of Creative Learning. Williamsville, NY: Center for Creative Learning.

Vehar, J.R., Shephard, W.J., Brese, C.A. (1995). The art of CPS facilitation. Buffalo, NY: Creative Education Foundation.

Vehar, J.R, Lunken, H.P., Brese, C.A., & Shephard, W.J. (1995). The art of facilitation. Buffalo, NY: Creative Education Foundation.

Vehar, J.R. (1994). CPS toolbook for group facilitators. (Unpublished manuscript available from Jonathan Vehar, New & Improved, P.O. Box 7043, Santa Monica, California 90406.)

Glossary

Client • *n.* The client is the person who convenes the problem-solving session, is accountable for the challenge, and is responsible for taking action.

Converge • *v.* To select among many options, to narrow down the choices

Creative Problem Solving (CPS) • *n.* A structured method of problem solving that leads to innovative, creative solutions

Diverge • *v.* To generate many options, to stretch beyond the obvious

Facilitator • *n.* The individual(s) who manages the process, but does not own the challenge

Highlighting • *n.* A three-step convergent tool for selecting among many options; the steps:
HITS: Identify options that are interesting, useful and will solve the problem.
CLUSTER: In order to avoid duplication, group "hits" that relate to each other.
RESTATE: Paraphrase the cluster in a way that synthesizes and captures the essence of the ideas.

Mind set • *n.* The unique thinking skill associated with each step of the creative process.

Ownership • *n.* (In regards to problem solving) being accountable for implementing or authorizing a solution to the challenge; The client is the "owner" of the problem.

Praise First (POINt) • *n.* A four-step technique used to evaluate and improve ideas, products, actions or options
PLUSES: what you like about it
OPPORTUNITIES: possible spin-offs
ISSUES: the drawbacks, phrased as questions to invite solutions
NEW THINKING: a brainstorm of new ideas to address each issue of concern

Resource Group • *n.* The people who help the client generate options and ideas; The resource group gives energy, enthusiasm and insight to help solve the challenge.

Statement Starters • *n.* Phrases that begin sentences; Different statement starters are used for each stage of the problem solving process. For example: *How to... , How might... , In what ways might..., It would be great if..., What I see myself (us) doing is...*

Notes:

Notes: